THE 2ND WORLD WAR

Fiona Reynoldson

Heinemann

Heinemann Educational,
a division of Heinemann Publishers (Oxford) Ltd,
Halley Court, Jordan Hill, Oxford OX2 8EJ
OXFORD LONDON EDINBURGH MADRID
ATHENS BOLOGNA PARIS MELBOURNE
SYDNEY AUCKLAND SINGAPORE TOKYO
IBADAN NAIROBI HARARE GABORONE
PORTSMOUTH NH (USA)

© Fiona Reynoldson

The moral rights of the proprietors have been asserted

First published 1993

British Library Cataloguing in Publication Data is available from the British Library on request.

ISBN 0-435-31672-9

Designed by Ron Kamen, Green Door Design Ltd, Basingstoke

Illustrated by Phill Burrows, Jeff Edwards and Peter Hicks

Printed in Spain by Mateu Cromo

The front cover shows Winston Churchill with a 'Tommy' gun, and a US tank.

Acknowledgements

The authors and publisher would like to thank the following for permission to reproduce photographs:
Associated Press: Cover; Bilderdienst Suddeutscher Verlag: 4.3D; Bridgeman Art Library/Imperial War Museum: 1.1A; British Library: 1.2A; Centre for the Study of Cartoons and Caricature: 3.2C; Centre for the Study of Cartoons and Caricature/David Low/Solo Syndication: 4.8D; Collection of Gunn Brinson: 1.4A; E. T. Archive: 1.1C, 4.3A, 4.7F; Mary Evans Picture Library: 1.4F, 4.7A; Hulton-Deutsch Collection: 1.4G, 2.5E, 4.4D, 4.6C; L'Illustration/Sygma: 2.2A; Imperial War Museum: 2.7A, 3.1A, 3.3A, 4.1B, 4.3H, 4.4C, 4.5B; Library of Congress, Washington: 4.8C; National Air and Space Museum, Smithsonian Institution: 3.5D; Netherlands Photo Archive/Charles Breijer: 4.2C; Peter Newark's Military Pictures: Cover; Popperfoto: 1.4D, 2.2C, 2.3A, 2.5A, 4.5E, 5.1D; The Prado, Madrid © DACS 1993/Arxiu Mas: 2.4B; Sygma: p.56, p.57; Topham Picture Source: Cover, 3.2A; Weimar Archive: 1.4C, 3.4B.

We are also grateful to the following for permission to reproduce copyright material:
Collins Educational for Source 5.2A, taken from P. Moss, *History Alive*, 1977.

Every effort has been made to contact copyright holders of material reproduced in this book. Any omissions will be rectified in subsequent printings if notice is given to the publisher.

Details of written sources

In some sources the wording or sentence structure has been simplified to ensure that the source is accessible.

L.S. Amery, *My Political Life*, extract quoted in J. Wroughton, below, 2.6E
A. Bullock, 'Hitler, A Study in Tyranny', Oddhams, 1952: 4.7B
S. L. Case, *The Second World War*, Evans Brothers, 1981: 3.4A
B. Catchpole, *A Map History of the Modern World*, Heinemann Educational, 1982: 1.3A, 4.8A, 5.3C
Chris Culpin, *Making History*, Collins, 1984: 4.8F
Jacques Legrand, *Chronicle of the Twentieth Century*, Longman, 1988: 1.3B, 2.1E
B. Elliot, *Hitler and Germany*, Longman, 1966: 2.2D, 2.5D
History of the Second World War, Purnell, 1968: 3.5B, 4.2B
T. Howarth, *The World Since 1900*, Longman, 1979: 4.3E
Illustrated London News, April 1936: 2.3D, 2.3E
Illustrated London News, March 1939: 2.4C
Nigel Kelly, *The Second World War*, Heinemann Educational, 1989: 3.5C, 4.3B, 4.3C, 4.3G, 4.8G
Nigel Kelly and Martyn Whittock, *The Era of the Second World War*, Heinemann Educational, 1993: 1.1B, 2.6C, 4.7C
Peter Mantin, *The Twentieth Century World*, Hutchinson, 1987: 4.3F
Karl Marx, *The Communist Manifesto*, Penguin Edition, 1967: 1.4B
Mass Observation, files at Sussex University: 4.6D
C. K. McDonald, *The Second World War*, Blackwell, 1984: 3.5A, 4.4B
Peter Moss, *Modern World History*, Hart-Davis Educational, 1978: 2.3B, 5.2C
Novosti Press Agency, *Recalling the Past*, Moscow, 1985: 2.6C
Alastair and Anne Pike, *The Home Front: Oral and Contemporary Accounts*, Tressol, 1985: 4.5C
Fiona Reynoldson, *Evacuees*, Wayland, 1990, 5.3F
Fiona Reynoldson, *Prisoners of War*, Wayland, 1990, 4.1A
Fiona Reynoldson, *Propaganda*, Wayland, 1990, 4.7E
Fiona Reynoldson, *War in Europe*, Heinemann Educational, 1980, 2.2B
S. Saywell, *Women at War*, Costello, 1985, 4.2D
Joe Scott, *The World Since 1914*, Heinemann Educational, 1989: 5.1C, 5.2D
R. Seth, *Operation Barbarossa*, Blond, 1964: 3.2B
K. Shephard, *International Relations, 1919–39*, Blackwell, 1987: 1.4H, 2.1C, 2.1D, 2.4D, 2.7D, 2.7E, 2.7F
Paul Shuter and Terry Lewis, *Skills in History*, Book 3, Heinemann Educational, 1988: 4.8B
John Simkin, *Contemporary Account of the Second World War*, Tressel Publications, 1984: 4.2A, 4.2B, 4.3I
L. Snellgrove, *The Modern World Since 1870*, Longman, 1981: 2.5B, 2.6F, 5.1A, 5.1B
A. J. P. Taylor, *The Origins of World War Two*, Hamish Hamilton, 1963: 2.3C
The Times Atlas of the Second World War, 1989: 1.3C, 5.3B
Ben Wicks, *No Time to Wave Goodbye*, Bloomsbury, 1988: 4.5D, 4.5F
J. Wroughton, *Documents on British Political History 1914–1970*, Macmillan, 1973: 2.6D, 2.7B

CONTENTS

PART ONE   NO MORE WARS?
1.1	The First World War	4
1.2	The Price of Peace	6
1.3	The League of Nations	8
1.4	Power and Politics	10

PART TWO   STEPS TO WAR
2.1	The Japanese Attack on Manchuria	14
2.2	Adolf Hitler – the Growing Threat	16
2.3	The Italian Invasion of Abyssinia, 1935	18
2.4	The Spanish Civil War	20
2.5	The Rhineland and Austria	22
2.6	Peace at Any Price?	24
2.7	The Collapse of Peace	26

PART THREE   WORLD AT WAR
3.1	War in Western Europe, 1939–41	28
3.2	The German Invasion of Russia	30
3.3	War in the Pacific	32
3.4	The Allied Victories in the West	34
3.5	Victory in the Pacific	36

PART FOUR   WAR AND THE PEOPLE
4.1	Life in Nazi Europe	38
4.2	Opposition to the Nazis	40
4.3	The Holocaust	42
4.4	The Home Front	46
4.5	Evacuees	48
4.6	The Blitz	50
4.7	Propaganda	52
4.8	Why Did the Allies Win?	54
4.9	The Big Four	56

PART FIVE   PEACE BREAKS OUT?
5.1	A Divided Europe	58
5.2	The United Nations Organization	60
5.3	Refugees	62
Index		64

1.1 The First World War

A SOURCE

'Hell', a painting done at the time by a French artist. It shows a First World War battlefield.

The First World War ended in 1918. It was a terrible war. In total, 20 million people died.

Spending money on the war

After the war many countries were poor. They had spent all their money on buying guns, aeroplanes and ships.

Total war

The First World War was a **total war**. This means that everyone was affected in some way. Millions of soldiers fought and died. Women, as well as men, worked in factories making everything from guns to bandages. The war affected people in other ways, too. In some countries there was not enough food. Everyone was busy fighting or making guns, so farmers did not have enough farmworkers to grow food.

B SOURCE

Last night, for the first time since August 1914, there was no light of gunfire in the sky. The fires of hell have been put out.

Philip Gibbs, writing in 'The New York Times', November 1918.

C

SOURCE

A French poster of 1919. It shows the horrors of war and the destruction that it caused to France.

D

SOURCE

What the war destroyed.

Revolution

Shortage of food and dislike of the war were two reasons why there were revolutions in some countries. Soldiers **mutinied** in both France and Germany and there was a **revolution** in Russia.

After the war

Many areas of land were wrecked by the fighting. It cost a lot to rebuild the farms and the houses. Some people hated the war. They said it must never happen again. These people were called **pacifists**.

Questions

1. Copy the following paragraph, choosing one of the alternatives in *italics*.

   20/200 million people were killed in the First World War. *Governments/ people* were short of money because they had spent so much on the war. The war changed most people's lives. Many men had been in the *army/ garden*. More women had gone out to *work/the shops* than before.

2. **a** How many men can you see in Source A?
   b How many are wounded or killed?

1.2 The Price of Peace

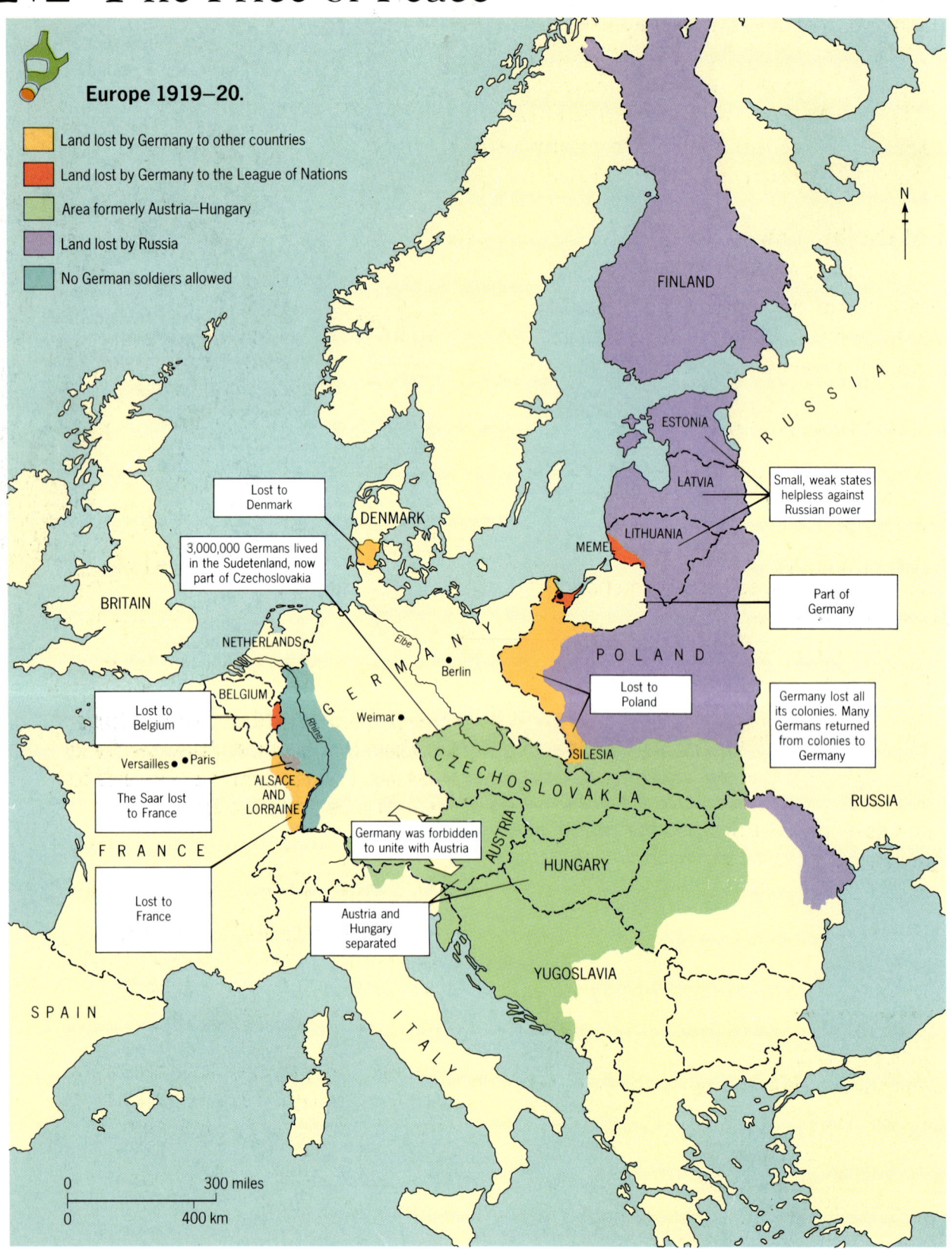

Europe 1919–20.

- Land lost by Germany to other countries
- Land lost by Germany to the League of Nations
- Area formerly Austria–Hungary
- Land lost by Russia
- No German soldiers allowed

Small, weak states helpless against Russian power

Lost to Denmark

3,000,000 Germans lived in the Sudetenland, now part of Czechoslovakia

Part of Germany

Lost to Poland

Germany lost all its colonies. Many Germans returned from colonies to Germany

Lost to Belgium

The Saar lost to France

Lost to France

Germany was forbidden to unite with Austria

Austria and Hungary separated

0   300 miles
0   400 km

6   THE ERA OF THE SECOND WORLD WAR

Making peace

The countries which had won the First World War were called the **Allies**. They did not want another war. They made a peace treaty. The peace treaty said two things. First, there must be no big **empires** in Europe any more. Second, Germany must be punished.

End of the big empires

The big empires of Russia, Germany, Austria-Hungary and Turkey had broken up during the war. The Allies made lots of small countries from the big empires.

The Treaty of Versailles 1919

The Treaty of Versailles was the peace treaty that ended the war. The Germans hated it. The treaty said:
1. The Germans started the war.
2. The Germans had to pay for the bombed houses and factories.
3. The Germans could only have a small army.
4. The Germans could not have any tanks, submarines or warplanes.
5. The Germans had to give up land and colonies.
6. The Germans must never unite with Austria.

The Price of War for France
250,000,000 cubic metres of trenches to fill in
320,000 km of barbed wire to pull up
300,000 houses destroyed
1,000 bridges blown up
6,000 factories gutted

SOURCE A

PEACE AND FUTURE CANNON FODDER

The Tiger: "Curious! I seem to hear a child weeping!"

A cartoon drawn in 1919. It shows the leaders of the Allies. They have just signed the Treaty of Versailles. Children born in 1919 would be old enough to be soldiers in 1940.

Questions

1. Read the first paragraph. Fill in the gaps. The countries which won the war were called the _____. The peace treaty said that _____ must be punished.

2. Read **The Treaty of Versailles** and the green box. Which country do you think would want to make Germany agree to No. 2 on the list?

3. Look at Source A and read the caption. Why is the child crying?

1.3 The League of Nations

Woodrow Wilson

Woodrow Wilson was the President of America. He wanted all the countries in the world to work for peace. He called this a **League of Nations**. So the League was set up in 1920 and over 50 countries joined it.

What the League of Nations hoped to do

Wilson hoped all the countries would help each other. If one country was attacked all the members of the League would refuse to trade with the attacker. The League also worked to stop other things like slavery and drug trading.

The League's successes – arguments

In 1920 Sweden and Finland argued. They both wanted the same piece of land. The League made them agree rather than fight about it. The League settled several arguments between countries.

SOURCE A

The League quickly turned into a talking shop, led by the countries which had won the First World War.

From B. Catchpole, 'A Map History of the Modern World', 1982.

How the League of Nations worked.

Secretariat
The permanent 'civil service' of the League. It carried out decisions taken by the Council.

General Assembly
Met once a year. All member nations of the League had one vote here.

Council of the League
A committee that took major decisions. Most European nations were members.

International Labour Organization
Each member nation sent two government ministers, one employer and one worker. They discussed working conditions and got countries to make improvements.

Court of International Justice
Fifteen judges met at The Hague in Holland. They settled international disputes, eg over frontiers or fishing rights.

Special commissions: drug addiction, health, slavery, help for undeveloped nations, refugees, minorities, mandates

The League's successes – for working people

The League set up the International Labour Organization. Its first director was a Frenchman. He was called Albert Thomas. He wanted to help all the working people in the world.

The League's successes – slavery

At the end of the war slavery was still legal in many countries. The League worked hard to stop this. They talked to governments. They pointed out how bad slavery was. By the 1930s slavery was illegal in most parts of Africa. It was still legal in some parts of the Middle East.

The League's problems – America

After the war Woodrow Wilson stopped being President of America. Wilson had worked hard for the League of Nations. But the new President was not interested. He felt everyone in America was fed up with Europe. So America did not join the League of Nations.

The League's problems – Russia and Germany

The Russians did not join the League of Nations for several years. Germany left the League in 1933. As America had not joined either, this meant that three big countries did not really support the League.

The League's problems – no teeth

The League of Nations was like a big lion with no teeth. It had no way to make people do what it said. For instance, in 1923 Lithuania attacked and took the port of Memel from Germany. The League of Nations said Lithuania must give it back to Germany. Lithuania just said no. The League of Nations had no way to make Lithuania give Memel back. When people saw the League was not working they soon ignored it.

B SOURCE

Jan 16 1920: The League of Nations met for the first time today but the Americans were absent.

From 'Chronicle of the Twentieth Century', 1988.

C SOURCE

March 1933: Japan leaves the League of Nations. **October 1933:** Germany leaves the League of Nations.

From 'The Times Atlas of the Second World War', 1989.

Questions

1. Read **Woodrow Wilson**.
   a. Who was Woodrow Wilson?
   b. What did he want?
   c. How many countries joined the League of Nations?

2. Look at the picture on page 8.
   a. What did the General Assembly do?
   b. What did the special commissions do?

3. Read Source B. How does it show that the League was weak?

1.4 Power and Politics

A

A German Communist poster.

In the 1920s and 1930s, there were three main political ideas. That is, there were three main ways to rule a country. There was the democratic way. There was the communist way. There was the fascist way.

The Democratic way
Britain, France and America were ruled in a democratic way. People chose the leaders they wanted by voting.

The Communist way
Russia and Germany had communist parties. These groups believed that ordinary working men and women should rule factories, farms and even the country itself. Many people thought communist ideas were very fair.

The Fascist way
Italy and Germany had Fascist rulers. These rulers believed in having one strong ruler or leader. Benito Mussolini led Italy. Adolf Hitler led Germany.

B Working men of all countries unite!

From Karl Marx, 'The Communist Manifesto', 1848.

C

SOURCE

A German anti-Communist poster. It shows Communism bringing death and disaster.

Questions

1. Read the first paragraph. Fill in the gaps.
   In the 1920s and 1930s there were ____ main ways to rule a country. There was the ____ way, the ____ way and the ____ way.

2. Look at Source A. Which of the statements below are true?
   The poster is on the government's side.
   The government men are running away from the clenched fist.
   The poster is telling the people to overthrow the government.

3. Look at Source C. Write down all the ways that the poster is saying that Communism will bring death and disaster. There are at least four.

4. Read Source B. Does it support Source A or Source C?

Dictators

A dictator is a strong leader. He tells everyone what to do. He has a lot of power.

Dictators and Fascists

Fascists believed in dictators. They felt a strong leader made a strong country. Both Mussolini, in Italy, and Hitler, in Germany, were dictators and Fascists.

Dictators and Communists

Communists really wanted the working women and men to run the country. But it was difficult to set this up. There had to be someone giving the orders for the working women and men. In practice, dictators often ran Communist countries.

Communist revolts, 1918–19.

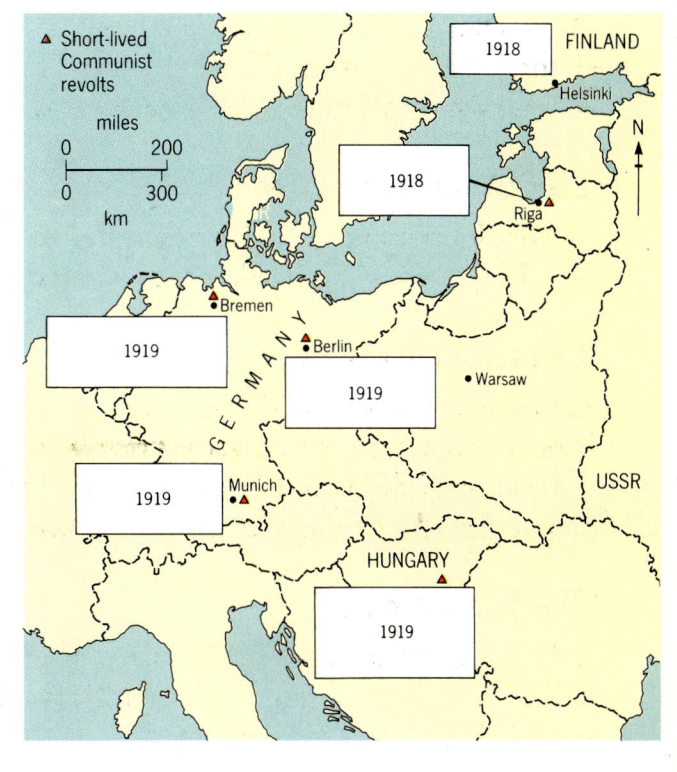

THE ERA OF THE SECOND WORLD WAR 11

SOURCE D

The leader of the Austrian Fascist Party at a rally in 1934.

The differences between Communists and Fascists

Both the communists and fascists said that a country needed a strong leader. But in other ways they did not agree with each other. Communists wanted all working men and women to work together to run the world under a strong communist leader. Fascists wanted a strong leader in their own country so that their country would be great.

Fascists and racism

Fascists were very proud of their country. But they went further than this. They thought their country was better than any other country. They thought that their race was better than any other race. This was called racism.

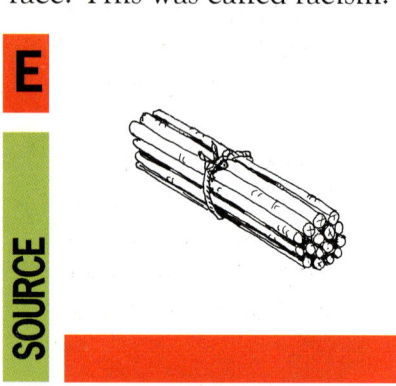

SOURCE E

The fasces that the Fascists took their name from.

SOURCE F

The cover of an Italian magazine, showing Hitler and Mussolini at a march in 1937.

12 THE ERA OF THE SECOND WORLD WAR

Mosley, the British Fascist leader, marching in Liverpool in 1937. Mosley is the man with his head in front of the banner.

SOURCE G

SOURCE H

Here I can arrest anyone that I want to and I can keep them in prison for as long as I want to.

This was said by the Head of the Portugese Secret Police.

The first Fascists
The first Fascists came from Italy. Their leader was Benito Mussolini. He led them from 1922 to 1943.

Other Fascists – the Nazis in Germany
The Nazi Party in Germany were Fascists. Their leader was Adolf Hitler. He led them from 1933 to 1945.

Where the Fascists failed
There were Fascist parties in other countries, like France. But the French did not want Fascist rule. In Britain, the Fascists were led by Oswald Mosley. They wore black shirts and went on marches. Few people in Britain liked Fascism.

The March of Fascism.

Questions

1. Read **Fascists and racism**. Fill in the gaps.
   Fascists were very ____ of their country. They thought their country was ____ than any other country.

2. Look at Source E. The bundle of rods was a sign of discipline and showed that a number of people sticking together were stronger than one person. Why might Fascists use this sign?

3. Look at all of the sources.
   a. Which show the Fascists kept power by frightening people about Communism?
   b. Which show the Fascists using marches and parades to keep power?

THE ERA OF THE SECOND WORLD WAR 13

2.1 The Japanese Attack on Manchuria

Japan needs land

In the 1920s and 1930s, Japan wanted more land. There were two main reasons for this:
1. The population of Japan was getting bigger and bigger. There was just not enough land for all the people to live on.
2. Japan did not have many raw materials like coal, iron, rubber and oil. The men who ran the factories in Japan wanted iron to make cars and machines. They wanted rubber to make tyres for bicycles, cars and trucks. Then they could sell these **goods** (the things they had made) and make money.

SOURCE A

– 1 Tonne

50 Tonnes

How much rubber was needed to build a tank and a destroyer.

Japan and China

Japan was a strong country, because it had a big, well trained army. China was weak. The country was big, and did not have a strong army. It did not have one strong leader. There were lots of leaders, each ran a different part of China. They argued and even fought with each other. All these things meant that it was easy for Japan to attack China.

1931

The Japanese army invaded the north of China. China asked the League of Nations for help. The League of Nations said that Japan was in the wrong. They hoped that Japan would leave China. But Japan left the League of Nations instead, in 1933.

SOURCE B

Dead and wounded Chinese after a Japanese bombing raid.

14 THE ERA OF THE SECOND WORLD WAR

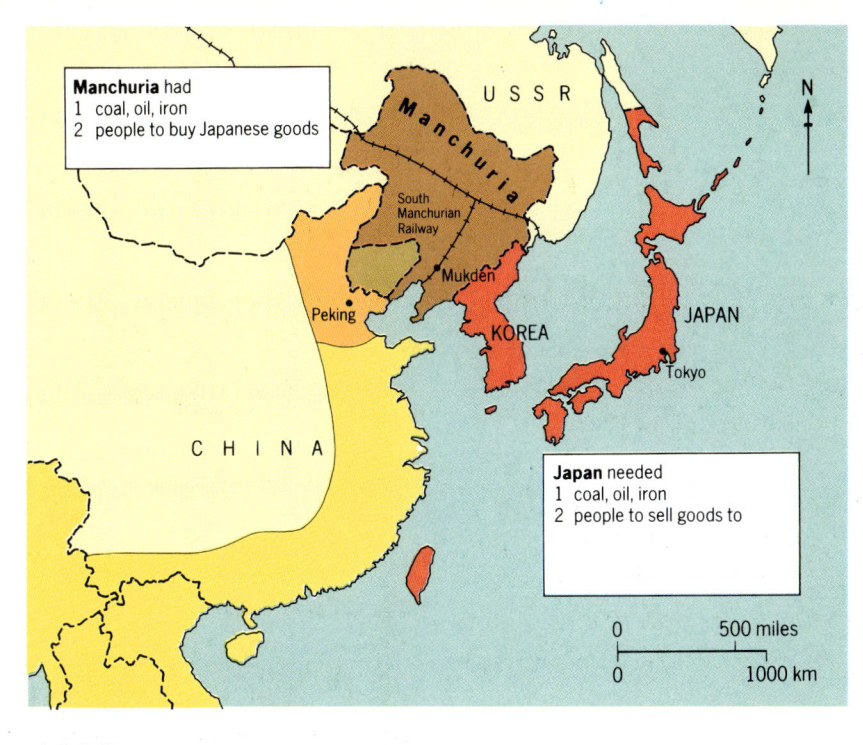

Japanese expansion in Asia in the 1930s.

Manchuria had
1 coal, oil, iron
2 people to buy Japanese goods

Japan needed
1 coal, oil, iron
2 people to sell goods to

Japan gets more land
- By 1920s
- 1931–2
- 1933
- 1935–6
- After 1937

1937

Japan then attacked the rest of China. Again China asked the League of Nations for help. But the countries in the League of Nations did not help. By 1938 Japan controlled most of east China (see map).

C Chinese troops damaged the tracks of the South Manchurian railway near Mukden.

Part of the Japanese Army report 1931.

D Japanese railway guards blew up part of the railway line near Mukden, and then blamed the Chinese.

Part of the Chinese Army report, 1931.

E "Japan has left (the League) with a heavy heart," said Mr. Matsuoaka. (The League said it was Japan who started the war over the Mukden railway.)

From Chronicle of the 20th Century, 1988.

Questions

1 Read the first paragraph. Copy the following sentences. Use one of the words in *italics* each time there is a choice. In the 1920s and 1930s Japan wanted more *people/land*. There were *two/six/four* main reasons for this. The population of Japan was getting *smaller/bigger*. Japan did not have enough coal, oil, rubber and *sand/iron* for the factories.

2 a Read Source C. Who damaged the railway?
   b Read Source D. Who damaged the railway?
   c Read Source E. Which side did the League of Nations believe?
   d What did Japan do?

2.2 Adolf Hitler – the Growing Threat

A SOURCE

Hitler meeting soldiers in the Saar in 1935.

Adolf Hitler

In January 1933 Adolf Hitler became the ruler of Germany. He was the leader of the Nazi Party, which was also called the National Socialist Party.

What Hitler wanted

Hitler wanted to make Germany great and powerful again. He wanted to build up a big army. He wanted Germany to have more land.

What Hitler did

Hitler took Germany out of the League of Nations because the League did not want Germany to be powerful again. As soon as Germany left the League, Hitler ordered the Germans to build new tanks, submarines, ships and warplanes. He also ordered that every young man had to have army training. He made the army much bigger and more powerful.

B SOURCE

People stood and listened to Hitler for two hours without moving. He told them he would make Germany great. He told them he would find them all jobs.

From Fiona Reynoldson, 'War in Europe', 1980.

16 THE ERA OF THE SECOND WORLD WAR

The Saar 1935

The area called the Saar had been taken away from Germany in 1919, after the First World War. In 1935 the people of the Saar voted to be ruled by Germany again. Hitler was pleased. It showed he was popular. The Saar also had lots of coal, iron and steel. This was useful for making guns and ships.

What the other countries did

Britain, France and Italy were worried about Germany. They agreed to stand together. But Britain broke the agreement. The British agreed to let Germany have a bigger navy. Then in 1936 the Italians fell out with the British and French too.

D

I am sure that Hitler does not want war.
(Lord Lothian)

What kind of man is this grim figure?
(Winston Churchill)

Hitler cannot get what he wants without war.
(Professor Roberts)

A pleasant person.
(G. Ward-Price)

SOURCE

British views of Hitler in the mid-1930s.

C

SOURCE

Hitler leaving the League of Nations in 1933.

Questions

1. Read the first and second paragraphs.
   a. Who became ruler of Germany in 1933?
   b. What did he want?

2. Read **The Saar 1935**.
   a. What did the people of the Saar vote to do in 1935?
   b. Give at least two reasons why this pleased Hitler.

3. Read Source D. Who was against Hitler?

4. Look at all the sources. Which one best shows that Hitler wanted the army's support? Explain why you think this.

2.3 The Italian Invasion of Abyssinia, 1935

A *An Italian photograph, taken in 1935, showing Abyssinians saluting their new ruler, Mussolini.*

Mussolini

Mussolini was the leader of Italy. He was a Fascist. He wanted to have a great empire. Italy already owned some land in Africa. Mussolini wanted more land to build his empire.

Abyssinia

Mussolini attacked Abyssinia in 1935. The Italians had been beaten by the Abyssinians in 1896. Mussolini used modern weapons, like warplanes and poison gas. The Abyssinians fought hard but many were killed. They needed help.

B You have to consider the value of the promise of the League that the independence of small states would be respected.

Said by the Abyssinian Emperor, Haile Selassie, to the League of Nations in 1935.

C The League died in December 1935. One day it was a powerful body, the next day it was an empty sham.

From A.J.P. Taylor, 'The Origins of the Second World War', 1961.

D All our aeroplanes are being used to bomb and machine gun this disorderly mob.

The Italian commander said this about the battle of Lake Ashangi, 1936, where the Italians beat the Abyssinians.

League of Nations

Abyssinia asked the League of Nations for help. The League said they would not sell any goods to Italy. This sounded good. However, the League said Italy could still buy some goods like steel and oil. This was hopeless. Steel and oil were just what Italy needed to make and run warplanes and ships.

Selling guns

Then the League decided not to sell guns to either Italy or Abyssinia. But Italy had lots of guns already. So it meant that Abyssinia could not get guns to fight back against Italy.

A deal with Italy

Britain and France wanted to do a deal with Italy. They promised Mussolini that he could keep the land he had already taken in Abyssinia, if he stopped fighting immediately. Ordinary people in Britain and France were shocked. They thought this was very unfair to Abyssinia. Britain and France backed down but it showed that neither Britain nor France would stand up to Italy. They were worried that Mussolini would turn to Hitler for help and that Italy and Germany would become close friends or allies.

Italy invades Abyssinia

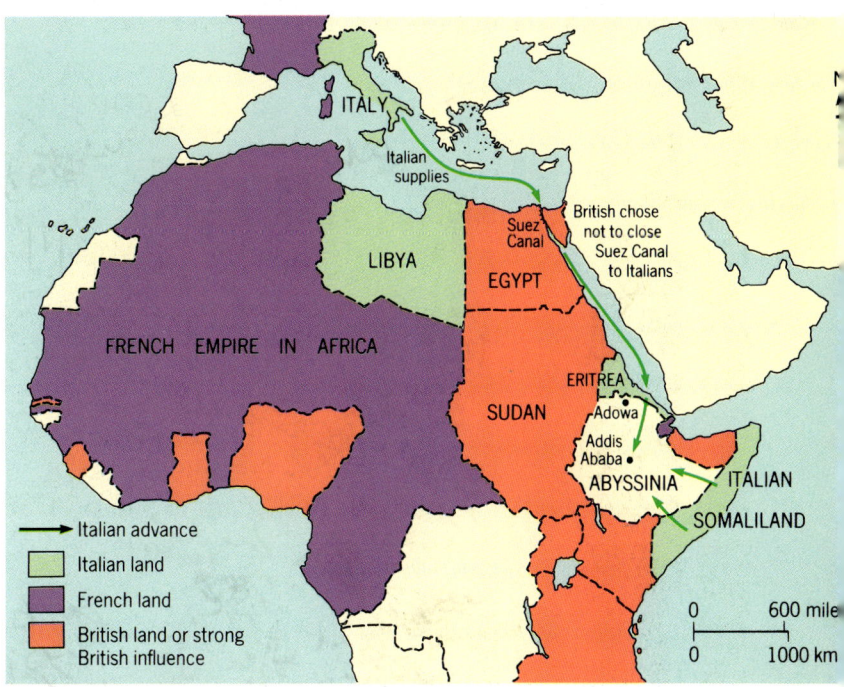

SOURCE E

The Abyssinian losses were described as heavy. Italian casualties were about 40 dead and wounded.

From the 'Illustrated London News', April 1936.

Questions

1. Look at the map on this page.
   a. How many countries owned land in Africa?
   b. About how far from Abyssinia was Italy?
   c. Why do you think Italy wanted Abyssinia?

2. Copy the sentences, matching Heads and Tails.
   Mussolini was the leader — empire.
   Italy already owned some — land.
   Mussolini wanted more — land in Africa.
   Mussolini wanted a great — of Italy.

3. Look at Source A. Do you think the photograph shows what really happened? Why?

2.4 The Spanish Civil War

Problems in Spain

In the early 1930s many people in Spain were discontented. A few rich people owned all the money and land. The poor had nothing. They wanted jobs and land. Many poor people wanted to change the government.

Communists, Socialists and Anarchists (Left wing parties)

Some poor people wanted a Communist government. All the land and jobs would be shared. No one would be very rich. Other people wanted a Socialist government. Only some land and jobs would be shared out. Some people could be richer than others. A few poor people were Anarchists. They did not want any government at all.

1936

In 1936 there were elections. Many poorer people voted for a left-wing government. The people in the government were a mixture of Communists and Socialists. They wanted to take land from the rich and give it to the poor.

SOURCE A

Germany sent warplanes to help Franco. So German pilots had a lot of experience when the Second World War broke out.

SOURCE B

The artist Picasso painted this picture in 1937. He called it 'Guernica'. Germans bombed the Spanish town of Guernica. Picasso was Spanish. He was not there at the time, but felt strongly about the attack.

THE ERA OF THE SECOND WORLD WAR

General Franco

In 1936 General Franco was the head of the army. He led the army on the side of rich people against the left wing government (Communists and Socialists). There was terrible fighting for three years.

The other countries

Britain and France kept out of the fighting in Spain. However, Russia helped the left wing government and the poor people. Germany and Italy helped Franco and the rich.

The end of the Civil War

General Franco won the Spanish Civil War in 1939. From then on he was the leader of Spain.

SOURCE C

General Franco entered Madrid without a shot being fired. Perhaps the most welcome sight to the people of Madrid were the lorries carrying food to the hungry crowds.

From the 'Illustrated London News', March 1939.

SOURCE D

Mussolini and Hitler saw Franco as a useful ally. Hitler also used the Spanish Civil War to test out German weapons.

From K. Shephard, 'International Relations 1919–39', 1987.

Areas captured by Franco & the Nationalists by February 1939.

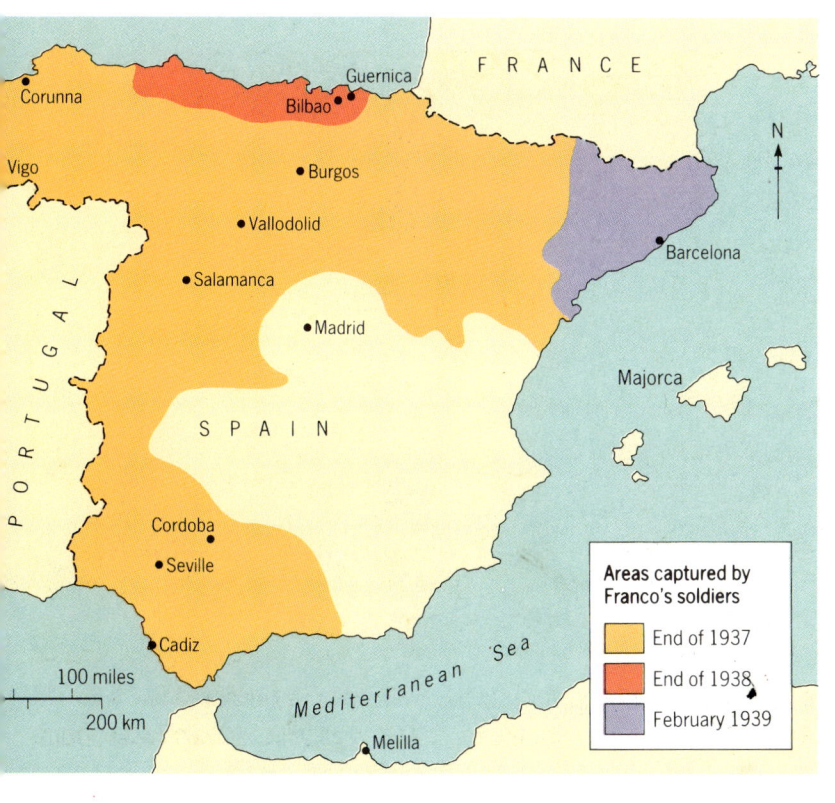

Areas captured by Franco's soldiers:
- End of 1937
- End of 1938
- February 1939

Questions

1. Read the first paragraph. Fill in the gaps.
   Many people in ____ were discontented in the early 1930s. The poor had ____.

2. Look at Source B.
   a. How many human figures are there?
   b. Choose two words which best describe what the people are feeling:
   pain   fear   joy   cold   hunger

3. Look at Source A. What new weapon did the Germans try out in Spain?

2.5 The Rhineland and Austria

A SOURCE

Crowds cheer as German soldiers enter the Rhineland, 7 March, 1936.

B SOURCE

The 48 hours after the march into the Rhineland were the most nerve-racking of my life.

Said by Adolf Hitler to one of his generals.

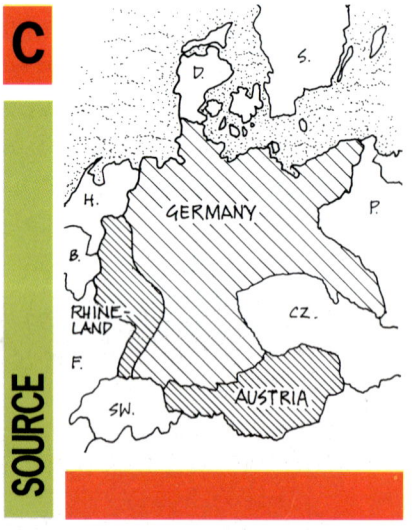

C SOURCE

Germany gets more land.

D SOURCE

Perhaps you will find me one morning in Vienna.

Said by Hitler to the leader of Austria, in 1938.

Keeping Germany weak

The countries which won the war wanted Germany to stay weak. The League of Nations wanted Germany to stay weak. There were several ways to keep Germany weak.
1 Germany was only allowed to have a small army.
2 Germany must never unite with Austria.
3 Germany was not allowed to have soldiers and forts in the area called the Rhineland, near the River Rhine. This was to stop Germany attacking nearby countries.

Hitler

Hitler wanted Germany to be strong. He made the army bigger. He built tanks and warplanes. The League of Nations did not stop him.

The Rhineland

Hitler got more daring. In 1936 he sent German soldiers into the Rhineland. The German people there shouted and cheered. Hitler held his breath. But the League of Nations did nothing.

Hitler and Italy

Next Hitler formed an alliance with Mussolini, the leader of Italy. Having got Italy's friendship he turned to Austria.

Hitler and Austria 1938

Hitler wanted to unite Germany and Austria. This would make Germany very strong. He invited the Austrian leader, Von Schuschnigg, to meet him. At the meeting he told the Austrian leader that Austria must become close friends with Germany and have Nazi party people in the Austrian government.

Germany took over Austria in 1938

Von Schuschnigg listened and went back to Austria. He decided to ask the Austrian people to vote on whether they wanted a close friendship with Germany. When Hitler heard this he was furious. He ordered Nazis in Austria to rebel. The Nazis forced Von Schuschnigg to resign. And on the 12 March 1938, German soldiers crossed the frontier into Austria. Some Austrians were pleased. Some were not so sure.

Questions

1. Read **Keeping Germany weak**. List the three ways that were used to do this.

2. Look at Source C. Which three countries were worried when Germany took the Rhineland? (S=Sweden, Cz=Czechoslovakia, F= France, Sw=Switzerland, P=Poland, H=Holland, D=Denmark, B=Belgium)

3. Look at Sources A and E. The photographers who took them were working for the German government.
   a. What do they show?
   b. Give two examples of things that they would not show.

E

Austrians cheer as German soldiers enter Vienna, 14 March, 1938.

2.6 Peace at Any Price?

Fear of war

In the 1930s many people were afraid of war. They still remembered how bad the First World War had been. So rather than stand up to Hitler, Britain and France let him have his way. This was called **appeasement** (trying to keep the peace).

Czechoslovakia 1938

Czechoslovakia was one of the countries next door to Germany. Part of Czechoslovakia was called the Sudetenland. Many Germans lived there (see map). Hitler wanted the Sudetenland to become part of Germany. Czechoslovakia wanted to keep it.

What Chamberlain did

The British Prime Minister at the time was called Chamberlain. He tried to sort the problem out. He talked to the Czechoslovakian leader, Benes. Benes said Germany could have the part of the Sudetenland where most of the Germans lived. Chamberlain thought that this seemed fair. He took this offer to Hitler. But Hitler said this was not enough. He wanted all of the Sudetenland.

Hitler got his way

On 28 September Chamberlain and several other leaders met Hitler. They said Hitler could have all of the Sudetenland. (No one had asked the Czech people what they thought.) Hitler was delighted. He said he would not ask for any more land. Everyone wanted to believe him.

SOURCE A
The British Prime Minister, Chamberlain, flew to Germany on 15 September 1938, to try to persuade Hitler not to fight (Czechoslovakia).

From N. Kelly, M. Whittock, 'Era of the Second World War', 1993.

SOURCE B

Chamberlain says Hitler has agreed to stop wanting more land.

SOURCE C
I felt it my duty to strain every nerve to avoid another Great War.

Said by Neville Chamberlain in 1938.

SOURCE D
We have been defeated. Czechoslovakia will soon be taken over by the Nazi regime.

Said by Winston Churchill in September 1938.

SOURCE E
Chamberlain had letters of congratulation from the king of the Belgians, and from thousands of ordinary people from all over the world. There would be no war.

From L.S. Amery, 'My Political Life', 1959.

How Czechoslovakia was divided in 1938.

- Given to Germany
- Seized by Poland
- Given to Hungary

F Chamberlain decided it was fair to give the Sudetenland back to Germany.

From L. Snellgrove, 'The Modern World Since 1970', 1968.

G To go into battle without our Empire behind us is unthinkable.

Said by Henderson, British Ambassador to Berlin, September 1938.

Cartoon bubbles (Why did Chamberlain choose appeasement?)

- Nothing to do with Britain
- Britain had too many possible enemies
- Hitler would soon stop making demands
- British army not ready for war
- Fear of Communist USSR

Why did Chamberlain choose appeasement?

Questions

1 Read the first paragraph. Copy out the right meaning of the word 'appeasement' from the list below.

1	Eating mushy peas
2	Getting angry
3	Giving in to keep peace
4	Pleasing a friend

2 Look at the cartoon opposite. Make a rough copy with the right number of bubbles.
Fill the empty bubbles with the ones you think are best from the list below.
Fear of war
Sympathy for Germans at Versailles Treaty
Dislike of loud noises
Fear the Empire will not help

THE ERA OF THE SECOND WORLD WAR 25

2.7 The Collapse of Peace

Hitler goes too far

Hitler thought he could take any land he wanted. He thought that no one would try to stop him. First he took over nearly all of Czechoslovakia in March 1939. Then, a week later, he seized Memel from Lithuania. Meanwhile, Hitler's ally, Italy, invaded Albania. Britain and France were horrified. They felt they could not trust Italy and Germany any more.

The Nazi-Soviet Pact: made between Germany and Russia

Things got worse. Germany and Russia signed an agreement (pact). This pact said that they would not be enemies. They would not fight each other. They would share Poland's land between the two of them.

A SOURCE

Welcoming the German soldiers.

B SOURCE

March 1939: Hitler took all of Czechoslovakia. Britain promised to defend Poland.

From J. Wroughton, 'Documents on British Political History', 1973.

C SOURCE

Tug-of-war over Danzig.

D SOURCE

There is no question of sparing Poland. There will be war. Our job is to isolate Poland.

Said by Hitler to his generals in 1939.

26 THE ERA OF THE SECOND WORLD WAR

Final steps to war, 1939.

Map legend:
- Germany by the end of 1938
- Seized by Germans, March 1939
- Seized by Hungary, March 1939
- Dominated by Germans
- Invaded by USSR, September 1939
- Invaded by Germans, September 1939

Map labels: FINLAND, SWEDEN, ESTONIA, LATVIA, LITHUANIA, USSR, Memel (seized by Germans, March 1939), Danzig (seized by Germans, Sept 1939), GERMANY, POLAND, CZECHOSLOVAKIA, AUSTRIA, HUNGARY

The invasion of Poland

On 1 September 1939, Germany invaded Poland. Britain and France had had enough. They saw that they would have to do something to stop Hitler. They saw that Hitler would not stop taking land unless he was forced to.

War at last

On 3 September 1939, Britain and France finally declared war on Germany.

SOURCE E

We will fight for Polish freedom. Every Polish house will be a fortress which the enemy will have to take by storm.

From a Polish newspaper, 1939.

SOURCE F

We secured peace for our country for one and a half years.

Said by the Russian leader, Stalin, to explain the 1939 Pact.

Questions

1. Read **The Nazi-Soviet Pact**. Fill in the gaps.
   Germany signed a pact with ____. They would not ____ each other.

2. Look at Source C. What town did Germany and Poland argue over?

3. Look at Source A. Choose the sentence which best describes the picture:
   The woman is crying with joy now the soldiers have come.
   The woman is sad because the soldiers have come.

4. Read **The invasion of Poland**. What effect did the invasion have?

THE ERA OF THE SECOND WORLD WAR

3.1 War in Western Europe, 1939–41

Poland and Blitzkrieg

The Germans attacked Poland. They bombed the Polish cities. Then the German tanks and soldiers moved in. On 24 September, 1,150 German planes bombed the city of Warsaw. The Russians attacked Poland too. The Poles did not have a chance. Germany and Russia divided Poland between them.

Britain and France get ready

Both Britain and France got ready for war. In Britain the government gave out gas masks and sent many of the children away from the cities. A **blackout** was ordered (blacking out windows and not using lights outside at night) so that German bombers could not see any lights from the air. In France, trains took thousands of people away from the area around the Maginot Line (see map). At the same time other trains took thousands of soldiers up to the Maginot Line.

Phoney war, real war

However, for months no bombers or German soldiers came. This lack of fighting made people call this the Phoney War. It didn't last. In April 1940, Germany invaded Norway and Denmark. Then in May, the German Panzer Tank Units crashed through the forests of the Ardennes and on into France.

The German invasion of France, May 1940.

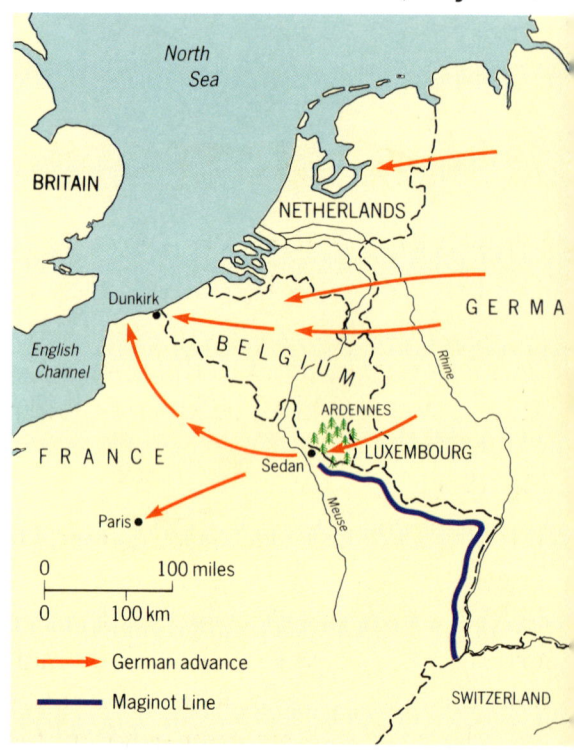

A SOURCE

A painting done at the time, showing the rescue of the soldiers from the Dunkirk beaches.

28 THE ERA OF THE SECOND WORLD WAR

SOURCE B

Date	Figures given by RAF in 1940	Figures given by RAF after war	Figures in German High Command Diary
15 August	185	76	55
18 August	155	71	49
15 September	185	56	50
27 September	153	55	42
Totals	678	258	196

Numbers of German aircraft shot down on the four days of the Battle of Britain.

French and British on the run

The British sent soldiers to help the French but soon 300,000 French and British soldiers were on the run. The Germans chased them to the port of Dunkirk. It looked as though they would all be killed or taken prisoner.

Dunkirk

The British decided to rescue as many soldiers as possible. They asked for help to get them off the beaches. Between 24 May and 4 June, hundreds of boats from fishing boats to ferries sailed across to France. The smallest boats sailed right up close to the beaches. The soldiers left their coats, held their rifles above their heads and waded out to the small boats. The small boats then took them to the big Royal Naval ships about a mile out to sea. Most of the thousands of soldiers were brought safely back to Britain. They could fight another day.

Would Germany invade Britain?

France surrendered and Germany took over most of France for the rest of the war. But would Germany invade Britain? Hitler knew he had to use his German airforce (the Luftwaffe) to destroy the British airforce (RAF) first. So a fierce battle went on in the skies over southern Britain all through the summer of 1940. Britain just managed to keep the German fighter planes out and by the end of the summer, Hitler gave up his plan to invade Britain. Instead he decided to bomb British factories and cities. He wanted to destroy the factories that made guns, warplanes and so on. He also wanted to frighten British people so that they would surrender. This bombing was called the Blitz.

Questions

1. Read **Poland and Blitzkrieg**. Fill in the gaps.
   The Germans attacked _____. First they bombed the _____, then the soldiers moved in.

2. Look at the map on page 28.
   a. What do the red arrows mean?
   b. What town did the Germans chase the British to?

3. Look at Source A.
   a. How did the British rescue their army?
   b. Find at least two signs of the Germans attacking.

4. Look at Source B. Which of the three different sets of figures of German planes shot down is most likely to be right? Why?

3.2 The German Invasion of Russia

Germany and Russia

Germany and Russia had signed a pact but Hitler did not like the Russians and he wanted some of their land.

Hitler invades Russia

In June 1941 German soldiers poured into Russia, speeding across the open spaces. The Russian soldiers retreated and retreated. By November the German soldiers were deep into Russia (see map). But the Germans were not prepared for the terrible Russian winter. Oil froze in the tanks, rubber tyres froze and the soldiers froze too. Many of them only had summer uniforms. Sometimes they almost froze to death. The German soldiers dug trenches and waited in them for spring. It was difficult to get food because the Russians had burnt all the farms and food as they retreated.

How the Russians coped

The Russians moved all their factories hundreds of miles to the east so they would be safe from the Germans. These factories poured out guns and other weapons as fast as possible. In one factory the big guns were loaded on to the trains unpainted. Women workers went on the trains painting the guns while the trains slowly made their way across the Russian countryside to the Russian soldiers at the front.

Spring and Stalingrad

After the winter the German soldiers continued to advance. They wanted to capture the oilfields in the Caucasus (see map). The Germans reached the city of Stalingrad but the Russians were determined to stop them there. They fought street by street to keep their city from the Germans.

A SOURCE

A German soldier using a flame-thrower to attack a Russian village.

B SOURCE

Rifles got so cold that if a man picked his up with his bare hand, the hand stuck to the rifle. It was so cold that he didn't realize what had happened. When he took his hand away the flesh of his palm and his fingers stayed on the rifle.

From R. Seth, 'Operation Barbarossa', 1964.

Winter and Stalingrad

The fighting went on for months. In November more Russian soldiers arrived and surrounded the Germans. Hitler said the Germans must fight on. But the German General, Von Paulus, said it was hopeless. He surrendered to the Russians in February 1943.

Result

The Germans lost about 200,000 soldiers. The Russians lost about 20,000,000 soldiers and civilians. These were terrible losses for the Russians, but the Russians had driven the Germans back. They had not been taken over by the Germans. The Germans had been beaten for the first time.

SOURCE C

A Russian cartoon showing Hitler ordering his soldiers to their death.

The German attack on Russia, 1941–2.

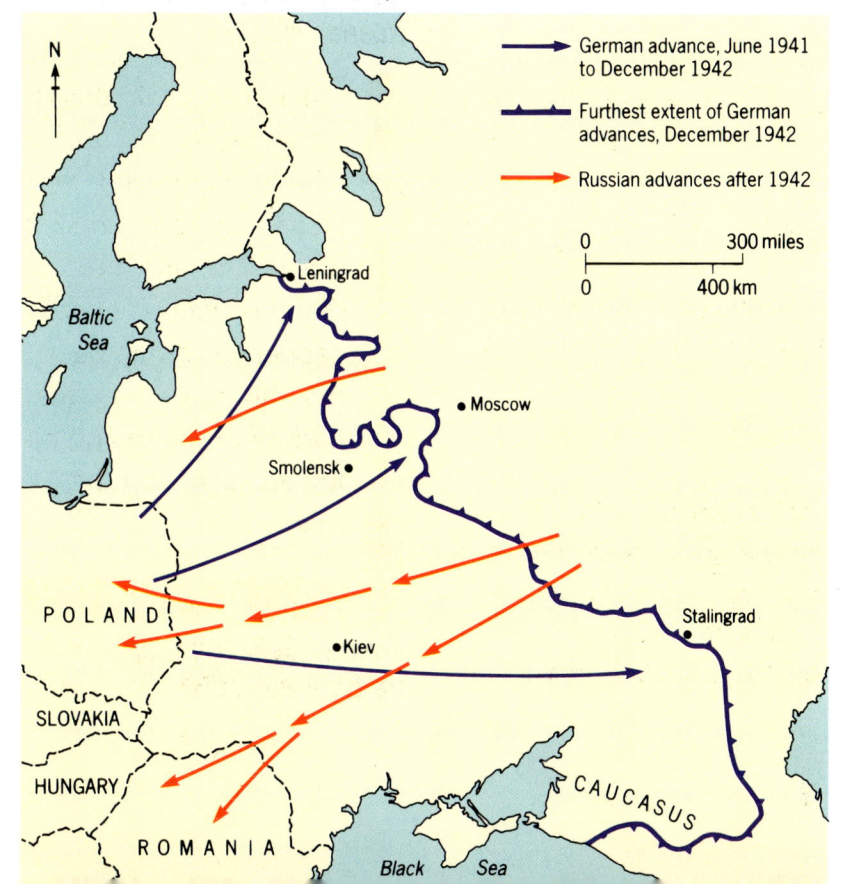

Questions

1. Read the first paragraph.
   a. What was the pact Russia and Germany had signed?
   b. Did Hitler like Russians?
   c. What did Hitler want?

2. Look at Source C. Write a sentence to explain how the artist shows that the soldiers are going to their deaths.

3. Read Source B. Does it agree or disagree with Source C? Why do you think this?

THE ERA OF THE SECOND WORLD WAR

3.3 War in the Pacific

The war spreads

By the end of 1941 the Second World War had spread across the world to the Pacific Ocean (the Far East).

Japan and the Far East

Europeans and Americans made lots of money trading with countries in the Far East. For instance, Britain and America got most of their rubber from Malaya. They made lots of money in the trade. Japan said this was unfair. However, Japan was not interested in the people of Malaya making money. Japan was more interested in making money itself. Japan wanted to control the Far East, all around the Pacific Ocean.

Japan and America

America did not want Japan to control the Far East. So America refused to sell any oil to Japan. This was a disaster. Japan got 80% of its oil from America. How could Japan run machines and factories? How could Japan make any trucks, tanks, bicycles or other machines at all?

1941

Japan decided to take land in the Far East. For instance, there was oil in the Philippines (see map). But the Japanese had to be careful. They had to be sure that the Americans did not use the American navy to stop them taking places like the Philippines. So Japan decided to knock out the American navy.

SOURCE A

A Dutch poster from the time. Before the war the Dutch had owned many of the islands shown on this poster.

32 THE ERA OF THE SECOND WORLD WAR

Pearl Harbor

The night of 6 December was beautiful. It was Saturday night and everyone at the American navy base of Pearl Harbor was looking forward to a fine Sunday. Many of the big American ships were anchored in the harbour. None of the American soldiers or sailors knew that the huge Japanese fleet was only 200 miles away. It was sitting silently in the moonlight waiting for dawn.

At 7.53 am next morning the first Japanese planes swooped on Pearl Harbor. They blew up ships and planes and killed over 2000 people. The Americans were angry and scared. The only good thing was that the big American aircraft carriers were at sea so they were quite safe.

Results

The Japanese had won for the moment. They went on to take more and more islands in the Far East. These included the British base at Singapore (see map).

SOURCE B

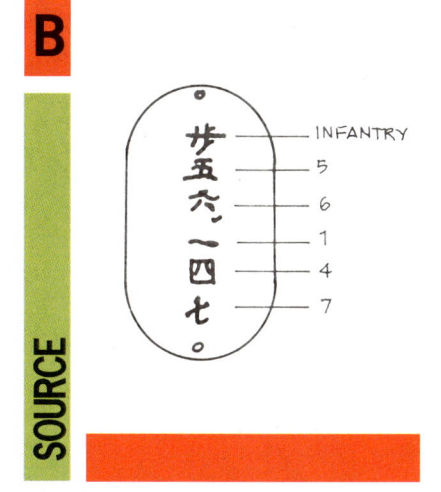

Soldiers of every army wore identity discs. Sometimes it was the only thing left when a soldier was killed. This Japanese soldier was in unit 56 and his own number was 147.

The war in the Pacific, 1941–2.

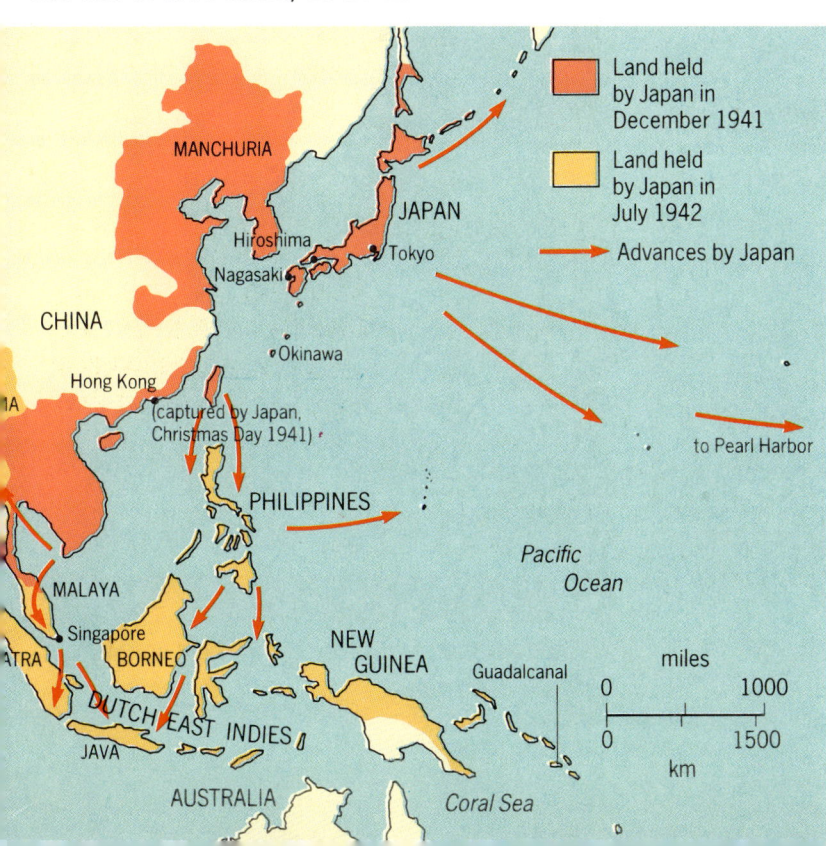

Questions

1. Read **Japan and the Far East**. Copy the following sentences. Use one of the words in *italics* each time there is a choice.
Americans/Africans and many Europeans made money trading in the Far East. Japan wanted to make *money/honey* itself. Japan wanted to control the *Near/Far* East.

2. Look at Source A. The red and white flag is Japanese.
   a. What animal is Japan shown as?
   b. Who made the poster?
   c. Do you think they liked the Japanese? Explain why you think this.

3.4 The Allied Victories in the West

By 1942 the Allies were made up of America, Britain, France and Russia. Now they were stronger than Germany. They started to win.

North Africa

The Suez Canal and the Mediterranean Sea were important to Britain. They were the way to the oil fields in the Middle East. Britain fought Germany and Italy to stop them getting to the Suez Canal. The British won at the Battle of El Alamein. From then on the British and the Americans worked together to push the German armies back.

Russia

From 1942 the Russians pushed the German armies back (see map on page 35).

France and D–Day, 6 June 1944

The Americans and the British sent thousands of soldiers to fight the Germans in France. They used 7,000 ships and landed 156,000 soldiers on the beaches on the first day (called D–Day). Someone said it was like moving the whole of a big city like Birmingham to France in one day. Every soldier had enough food for 24 hours. He carried everything from chewing gum to stop him feeling seasick, to spare socks and a rifle.

The soldiers fought the Germans and captured the beaches. Then more and more American and British soldiers were landed on the beaches. They fought their way inland. By September there were 2 million soldiers in France. Slowly, very slowly, they pushed the German soldiers back towards Germany (see map).

A SOURCE

In German cities people camped in the ruins with no light, heat or water, and had to scavenge like animals.

From S. L. Case, 'The Second World War', 1981.

B SOURCE

A Russian poster, encouraging their soldiers to fight the Germans.

Bombing

The British and the Americans bombed German cities. They sent as many as 1,000 bombers at a time. German cities like Dresden, Hamburg and Cologne were flattened. By May 1945, whole streets in Berlin were a mass of rubble and bricks. Many died in the bombing and in the fires which were so powerful they sucked people into the flames. Survivors lived in the cellars.

The end of the war in the West

In May 1945, the Russians reached Berlin from the east. The British, Americans and French reached Berlin from the west (see map). Hitler killed himself and Germany surrendered.

Questions

1 Read the first paragraph. Who were the Allies?

2 Look at the map on this page.
  a What are the red arrows?
  b What are the purple arrows?

3 Look at Source B
  a Who made this poster?
  b Choose a word from below to say how the soldier feels.
  happy sad fierce desperate determined calm brave

The defeat of Germany.

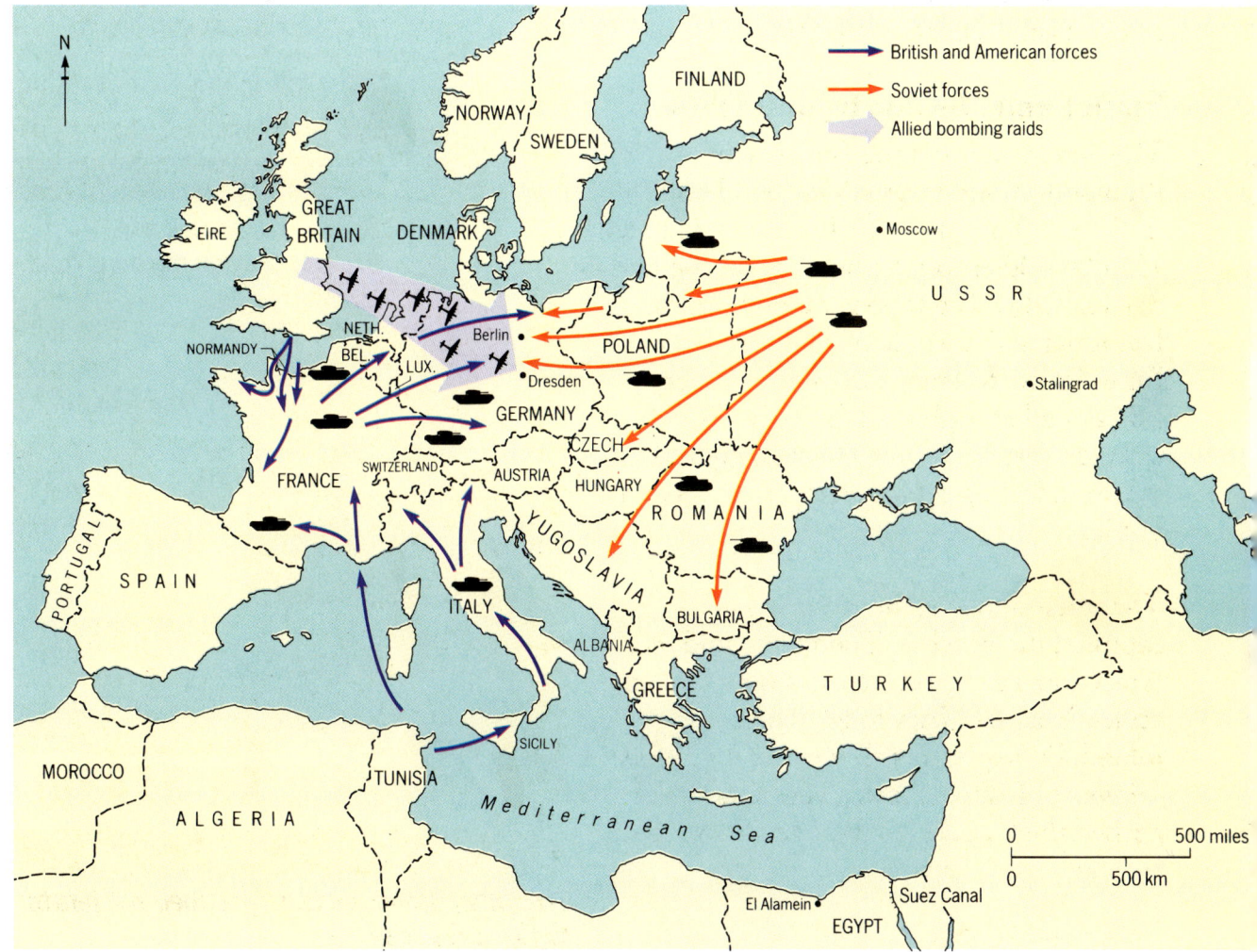

3.5 Victory in the Pacific

In 1942 Japan held lots of land in the Far East. But America was fighting back. The American navy won sea battles at Coral Sea and Midway.

Soldiers and kamikazes

America decided to capture one island at a time. Each time they got a little nearer to Japan. The Japanese fought very hard. Japanese people thought it was dreadful to surrender. If a Japanese soldier surrendered his family would not be given a pension.

On the other hand to die for Japan was a great honour. Young men queued up to be trained as suicide or kamikaze pilots. They flew planes loaded with bombs straight into the American and British ships. All the bombs blew up and the ships blew up as well.

America fights towards Japan

As 1943 and 1944 went by American soldiers got nearer and nearer to Japan. By mid 1945 the Japanese were in a desperate position. American bombers dropped fire bombs on cities like Tokyo. Thousands died.

A SOURCE
To be captured is a disgrace to the Army, your parents and your family. Always save the last bullet for yourself.

From the Japanese Army Manual issued during the war.

B
My God, what have we done?

Said by the bomber pilot who dropped the atomic bomb.

C
This is the greatest thing in history.

Said by the American President, when the bomb had been dropped.

D SOURCE

The city of Hiroshima after the atomic bomb had been dropped.

Would Japan surrender?

The Japanese thought of surrendering, but did not do so. The Americans wanted to make sure Japan was completely defeated and could not fight again. The Americans planned to invade Japan. But they knew the Japanese would fight to the death. The American government was worried that the American people would be against invading Japan because of this. How many of their soldiers would die?

The Atomic Bomb

The answer to the problem seemed to be the new atomic bomb. It was very powerful. No one really knew just how powerful it would be. It was top secret.

The American President sent a message to the Japanese. They must give up everything to the Americans. The Japanese did not reply.

Hiroshima

On the morning of 6 August 1945, an American bomber flew over the city of Hiroshima and dropped the very first atomic bomb. A huge mushroom cloud rose into the sunny sky. The bomber turned away. Below it the city of Hiroshima lay in ruins.

Nagasaki

The Japanese still would not surrender so the Americans dropped another atomic bomb, this time on Nagasaki. The Russians attacked in the north. Now the Japanese gave up. The war was over.

E SOURCE

My daughter had no burns. But then, on 4 September she got very sick. Her hair began to fall out, and she vomited clots of blood many times. Aften ten days of agony she died.

Said by a father in Hiroshima about his daughter's death.

Questions

1. Read the first paragraph. Copy the following sentences. Choose one of the words in *italics* when there is a choice.
In 1942 Japan had lots of *land/elephants* in the Far East. Then America started to win some famous *land/sea/air* battles. One of these was the Battle of *Halfway/Midway*.

2. Read **America fights towards Japan** and **Would Japan surrender?**.
   a. Who was in a bad position by 1945?
   b. What did the Japanese think of doing?
   c. What did the Americans want to be sure of?

3. Look at Source D. Read Sources B and C. Which source do you agree with? Why do you think this?

4.1 Life in Nazi Europe

By the end of 1942 Germany controlled most of Europe. The only countries that stood against Hitler were Russia and Britain.

What Germany got

As soon as German soldiers had conquered a country, they took everything they could. They took food, coal, oil, shoes, machines, art treasures and clothes. For instance, France was famous for beautiful clothes. When the Germans conquered France they sent train loads of French silk stockings back to Germany. For a while the German shops were full of silk stockings.

Slave workers

People were taken too. Germany needed millions of people to work on farms. By 1944 there were seven million slave workers in Germany. Many of these were Russians who had been captured.

SOURCE A

The starving Russian prisoners passed in endless columns. Those who could not keep up were shot. We spent the night in a small village and saw how, at night, the prisoners roasted and ate those of their fellows who had been shot.

From Fiona Reynoldson, 'Prisoners of War', 1990. Quoted by Dr Faulhaber.

Europe at the end of 1942.

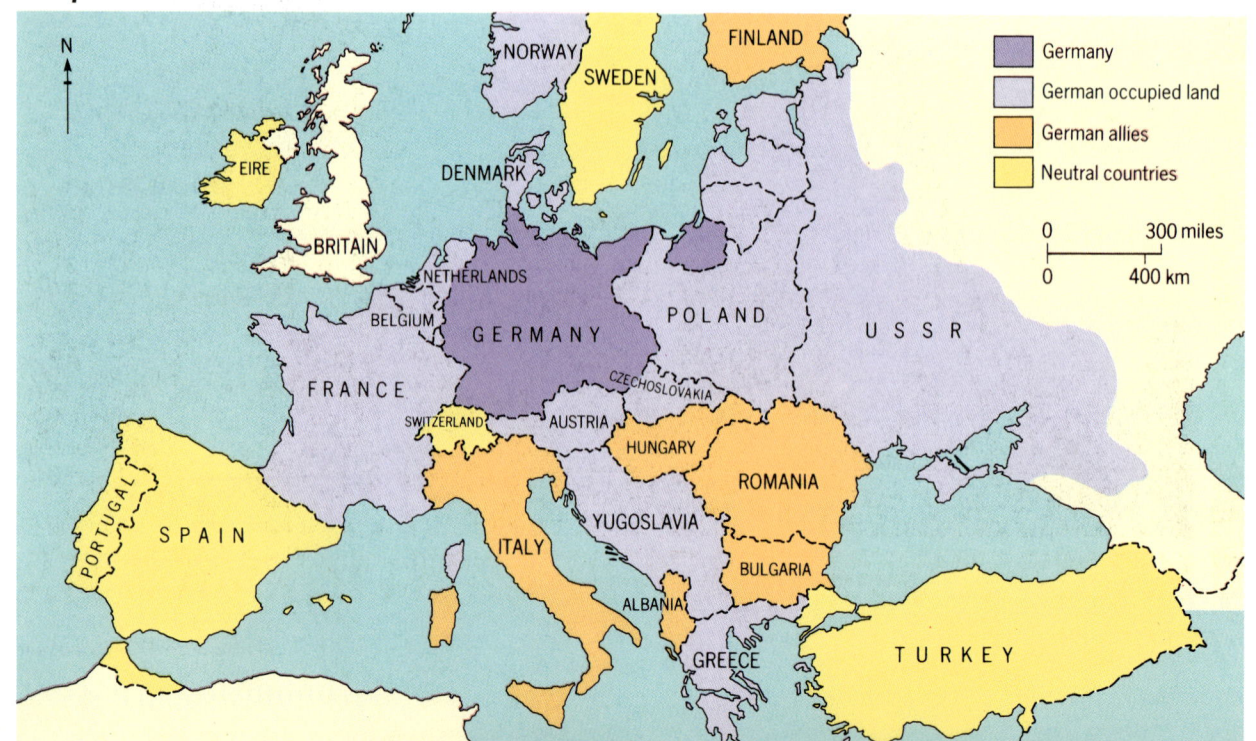

Western Europe

The Germans treated the people of western Europe quite well. In Norway and France they let local men rule. However the Germans used the Gestapo (secret police) and the SS (Schutz-Staffeln – Hitler's own army) to make sure that everyone obeyed. The local men were only allowed to run the country as long as they ran it in the right way.

Eastern Europe

The people who supported the Nazis in Germany looked down on Russians, Poles and all the other people that Germany had conquered. They killed thousands of these people. In some parts of Russia it is estimated that the Nazis killed at least one person out of every four people. No one knows for sure. Whole villages were burnt. The Nazis wanted the land cleared so that German people could farm it.

Questions

1 Read **What Germany got**. Make a list of the things that Germany took from other countries.

2 Look at the map on page 38. Make a list of the countries that Germany took over.

3 Read **Eastern Europe**. Choose the two reasons that best explain why the Germans treated the Russians badly:
The Germans were cleverer.
The Germans wanted the land.
The Germans looked down on the Russians.
The Germans were careless.

German soldiers hanging Russians.

4.2 Opposition to the Nazis

How the Germans felt about Hitler

At first Hitler was popular in Germany. He had made Germany rich and great again. He had made lots of jobs for Germans. Most people closed their eyes to other things that Hitler did, like getting rid of trade unions and persecuting Jews.

What happened to people who didn't like the Nazis?

Some Germans spoke out. They said that Hitler should not harm the Jews or anyone else. Hitler did not tolerate this. Anyone who spoke against him was arrested and often killed.

Resistance

In the countries that the Germans had conquered many people hated the Nazi rule. Some of these people carried on a secret war against the Germans. They were called the Resistance. They did as much as they could to fight the Nazis. They put bombs on railway lines, so that German soldiers and goods could not be moved so easily. They printed secret newspapers with lots of stories against the Germans. They helped Jews and others to escape. There were resistance groups like this in France, Poland and other countries.

Anyone caught resisting the Germans was killed. Sometimes his or her whole family or even the whole village was killed too.

SOURCE A

Dear Parents: bad news, I have been condemned to death. Gustav and I did not sign up for the SS. Both of us would rather die. I know what the SS have to do. We do not want to do it.

Written by a German farm worker in prison.

SOURCE B

First they came for the Jews
– and I did not speak out -
because I was not a Jew
Then they came for the communists
– and I did not speak out -
because I was not a communist
Then they came for trade unionists
– and I did not speak out -
because I was not a trade unionist
Then they came for me -
and there was no one left
to speak out for me

A poem written in prison by Pastor Niemoller, a German churchman.

C

SOURCE

A woman taking a secret photograph. She is pretending to look for something in her bag. The lens of the hidden camera is just below the centre of the two rings of the bag.

D

SOURCE

We helped some Soviet prisoners to escape. Poor people. They were forced to clear mines (bombs) from the minefield by walking in a line with linked arms over the field.

From S. Saywell, 'Women at War', 1985. Said by Carla Capponi.

The Allies and the Resistance

The Allies wanted to defeat Germany. So they helped the Resistance in places like France. In 1940, Britain formed a Special Operations Executive (SOE). The SOE trained men and women to go secretly into countries that the Germans had taken over to help the Resistance in those places. One way they could help was to find out where the big guns were, or where lots of soldiers were. All the information that they collected helped the Allies when they invaded Europe on D–Day.

Questions

1. Read the first and second paragraphs. Fill in the gaps. Hitler was popular in _____. He had made lots of ____. People tried to forget that he also persecuted ____. The Germans who spoke against him, were _____ or killed.

2. Read Source B. Choose the sentence which best describes what it means:
You should not interfere.
You should always think of yourself first.
You should speak out for what is right.

4.3 The Holocaust

Aryan people

Hitler said that Germans and other people in north Europe were Aryans. He said Aryans were the master race. They should rule the world.

Jews

Hitler and the Nazi Party hated anyone who was not Aryan. They hated the Jews most of all. Hitler said that the Jews were to blame for everything bad that happened. Then he said that the Jews were also to blame for everything bad that had ever happened to Germany in the past. He went on and on in his speeches about how bad the Jews were until, in the end, many ordinary Germans began to believe the things he said about the Jews.

Shops, jobs and public places

Nazi soldiers smashed Jewish shop windows. Jews got beaten up by soldiers more and more often. Then, in 1933, all Jews were thrown out of government jobs.

Worse and worse

In 1935 Jews were banned from using public swimming pools and parks. Non-Jews were not allowed to marry Jews. Things got worse and worse. Hitler and the Nazis began to pick on people who were only partly Jewish. People who were half or a quarter Jewish were told they were Jews. Many people found out that their grandmother or great-grandfather had been Jewish. They were terrified.

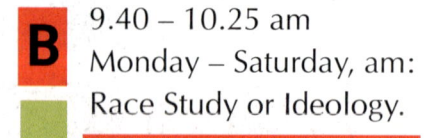

A *A Nazi poster, showing the Germans clearing out the 'muck' – Communists and Jews.*

B 9.40 – 10.25 am Monday – Saturday, am: Race Study or Ideology.

From a German school timetable in the Nazi period.

C When I went to school, aged 10, a third of my classmates were Jewish girls. I got on just as well with them as with the other girls. But we were told that the Jews were all wicked.

Said by a German woman who went to school in the Nazi period.

9 November 1938

On 9 November 1938 a German was murdered in Paris, and a Jew was blamed. The Nazi Party sent soldiers to punish all the Jews they could find. The soldiers burnt homes and synagogues (places where Jewish people worship) and smashed shops.

Concentration camps

Over 30,000 Jews were sent to concentration camps. These were prison camps for people who the Nazis did not like. The Jews joined everyone else who Hitler disliked, or who had stood up to him. After this many Jews ran away from Germany.

SOURCE D

A cartoon showing an anti-Jewish lesson. The pupils are being taught what were seen as signs of Jewishness.

SOURCE E

In 1934 a schoolboy in Berlin said "My Daddy says that not all Jews are vile." His daddy was put in prison.

From T. Howarth, 'The World Since 1914', 1979.

Questions

1. Read the first paragraph. What was the name that Hitler gave the 'master race'?

2. Read **Jews**. Choose the sentence which best explains how Hitler got so many Germans to believe the Jews were bad:
   Hitler kept quiet about Jews.
   Hitler wrote 20 books.
   Hitler kept on saying that the Jews were bad.

3. Look at Source D.
   a What does the picture the boy is pointing to show?
   b What does Source D tell you about Nazi schools?

4. Look at Source A. Why do you think the Nazis made this poster?

Ghettoes and concentration camps

The Germans treated the Jews badly in each country they conquered. Sometimes Jews were shut up in separate places inside cities (ghettoes). Often the Jewish children, women and men starved. Other Jews were sent to concentration camps where they were put to work. They were often worked to death.

The Holocaust

Hitler decided on a Final Solution to the Jewish 'problem'. It meant killing all the Jews. It has become known as the Holocaust.

Six million Jews were killed. Some were shot but this was too slow for the Nazis. They built big halls (chambers) at some camps. They sent up to 2,000 Jews into them. Sometimes they gave each person a bar of stone which they said was soap. The Jews thought they were going for a wash. They went into the chamber. The doors were sealed. Gas was put into it. In three minutes everyone was dead. The bodies were burned.

Experiments

At other camps Jews were used for medical experiments, often without **anaesthetics**. Most of them died.

SOURCE F Hitler has ordered that every Jew that we can lay our hands on is to be destroyed now, during the war, without exception.

Written by Rudolf Hess, Commander of Auschwitz Concentration Camp.

SOURCE G Then the prison guards had to find the small children who had been hidden. They opened the doors of the gas chamber and threw the children in. "It's terrible," I said. "You get used to it," he said.

An SS officer, interviewed on TV in the 1960s, talking about first seeing Jews gassed.

The main concentration camps.

The end of the war

When the Allied soldiers saw the concentration camps they were horrified. They vomitted at what they saw. They took photographs and films to show all the world what had happened to stop it ever happening again.

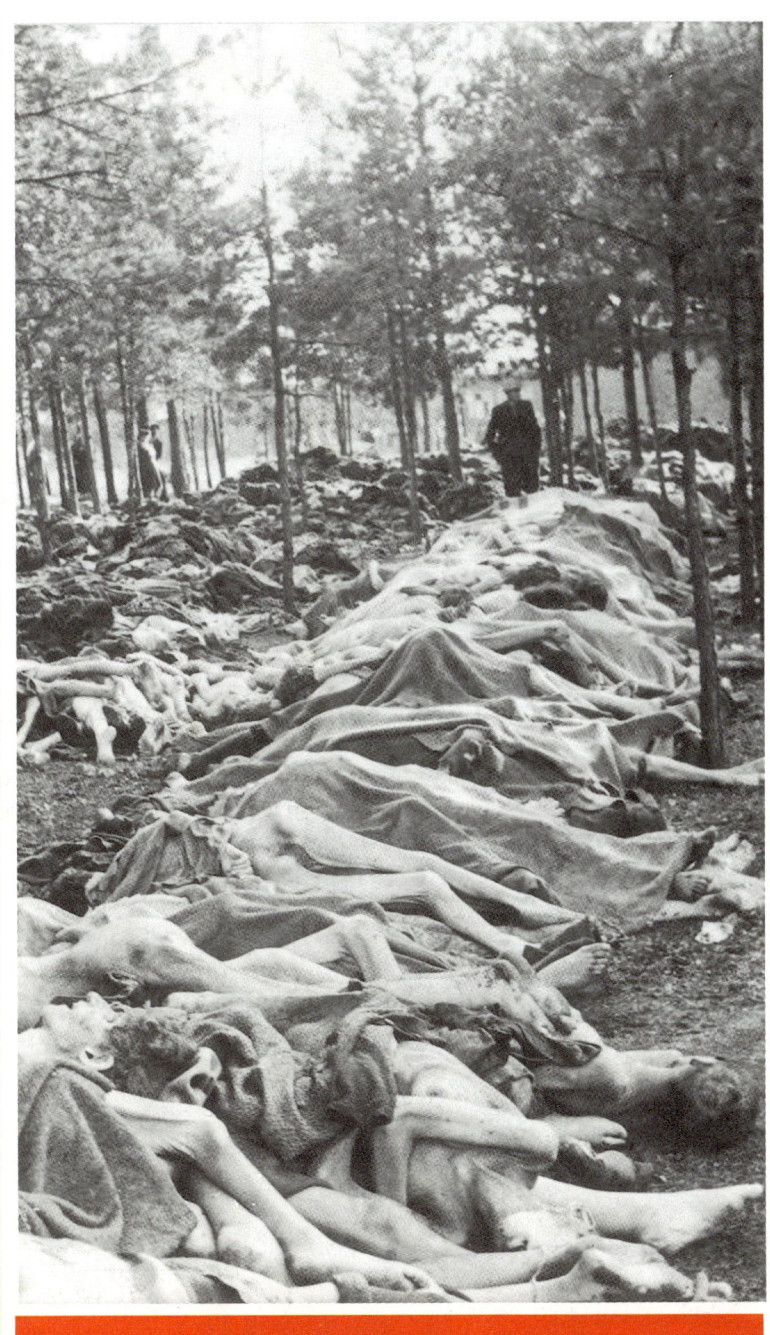

H SOURCE

Rows of corpses waiting to be buried at a Nazi death camp.

I SOURCE

It is the greatest mass killing in history, and it goes on daily, hourly. I have been talking to Allied troops about this for three years now, and it is always the same. They don't believe it.

Written by A. Koestler, an American journalist, in the 'New York Times', 1944.

Questions

1 Read **The Holocaust**. Fill in the gaps.
   The Holocaust was the killing of ____ million Jews by the Nazis. Some were ____. Others were herded into ____ and gassed.

2 Read Source G. The writer was a Nazi. Choose the sentence which best explains why he was still shocked by what he saw:
   He was a kind man.
   He was a weak person.
   He was seeing the gassing for the first time.
   He was lying in the 1960s.

3 Read **Experiments**. How did the Nazis feel about the people they did this to?

4.4 The Home Front

Many men between the ages of 18 and 41 went to fight. This changed the lives of everyone very much.

Women and the war

The war changed women's day to day life greatly. Often the men of the family were away. Women were running the family and often doing a job on their own.

Running the family and rationing

Most of Britain's food came from other countries by ship. During the war many ships were sunk. So Britain was short of food. Food was rationed (shared out among everyone). Everyone in Britain had a ration card. This was very fair. But mothers now had to cope with rationing. They had to make a little food do lots of meals. Sometimes there was so little food that women had to queue for hours to get one piece of fish. This took up a lot of time all through the war.

Women out at work

Many men went to fight. So the government wanted women to work in the factories and on the farms. In 1940 all women under 50 years of age had to go out to work (unless their children were under 14 years old).

A SOURCE

Milk 1.7 L.
Sugar 225 g.
Coffee 55 g.
Jam 115 g.
Cheese 85 g.
Meat 1s. worth
½ Egg

One person's rations for one week.

B SOURCE

Most people are better fed than they used to be. Rationing has increased the amount of milk that people drink.

George Orwell talking about rationing at the time.

C SOURCE

A wartime painting of a woman doing a skilled job using complicated machines.

Farms

By 1943 there were nearly 80,000 women in the Women's Land Army. They joined the Land Army to do the work of the men who had gone to war. They drove tractors, milked cows, planted potatoes and dug ditches. Most of the women enjoyed the work.

Factories

Many women worked in factories. They were always paid less than men for the same job, but many had their own money for the first time in their lives. They liked it. Some women at factories like Rolls Royce went on strike for equal pay with men. They said that the women doing **skilled work** on the machines were only paid the same as the unskilled men who cleaned the lavatories. Was this fair? At last the women got paid more money (but still not as much as skilled men).

Women's Voluntary Service

Older women often joined the WVS. These women did everything from driving ambulances, running canteens at railway stations, running nurseries for working mothers to knitting socks for sailors and collecting metal to make aeroplanes.

Dad's Army (the Home Guard)

Older men often joined the Home Guard. After work they went off to train as soldiers in case Britain was invaded. When they weren't doing that they were digging their gardens to grow as many vegetables as possible to feed the family.

D SOURCE

Wartime women on a protest march.

Questions

1. Read **Running the family and rationing**. Copy the sentences below, matching the Heads and Tails.

Women queued for hours	by ship.
Every person in Britain	sunk.
Most of Britain's food came	had a ration card.
Food was shared out among	for a piece of fish.
Many ships were	short of food.
Britain was	everyone.

2. Look at Source A. List how much of each thing you could have then. List what you eat in a day now.
   a How much more or less than the rations do you eat now?
   b What else do you eat?
   c How much of this comes from other countries (probably by ship)?

4.5 Evacuees

As soon as the war started the government knew cities would be bombed. They asked parents to send their children away from the cities. This was called **evacuation**. On Friday 1 September 1939 thousands of families were packing bags. Mothers and children were crying. Parents waved goodbye to their children. They did not know if they would ever see them again.

School children went with their schools. Children under five went with their mothers. Hundreds of trains took the children to the country. Each train carried about 800 children. None of them knew where they were going. The children were met at the station. Local people took them into their homes. Some children settled down happily. Many did not. They were homesick. The country people had to put up with a lot too. They took strange children into their homes. Some children were in rags. Some were dirty. Some were very naughty.

No bombs fell at first so by Christmas nine out of every ten children went home. Later when the bombs came, many did not leave the cities again. However, sometimes whole schools were evacuated and stayed in the country for the whole war. Some children were even evacuated as far away as America or Canada for the whole war.

SOURCE B

A government poster from the Second World War.

SOURCE A

This drawing shows children leaving a big city.

SOURCE C

Everything was so clean. We were given toothbrushes. We'd never cleaned our teeth until then. And the hot water came from a tap. And there was a toilet upstairs. And carpets. This was all very odd. I didn't like it.

Memories of a Second World War evacuee.

D SOURCE

This drawing shows children arriving in the country.

E SOURCE

Children on their way to the countryside, 1938.

F SOURCE

I looked out of the window and I saw my mother crying outside. I said to my brother "Why is mummy crying?" He told me to shut up.

Memories of a Second World War evacuee.

Questions

1. Read the first paragraph. Fill in the gaps.
   When the war started the government knew the cities would be _____. They wanted to send the _____ away from the cities. This was called _____

2. Look at Sources A and D. Write a sentence for each picture to explain what is happening.

3. Look at Source E.
   a. Choose one word from the list below to describe how the children feel.

   sad   happy   upset   worried
   lost   scared   frightened   OK

   b. Which child in Source E might have memories like the child in Source C? Explain why you think this.
   c. Do you think Source C is more or less reliable than Source E? Explain why you think this.

THE ERA OF THE SECOND WORLD WAR   49

4.6 The Blitz

In September 1940 Hitler gave up his plans to invade Britain. He decided to bomb the cities instead.

The big bombers

The bombing started on 7 September and went on for months. Night after night people heard the wail of the air raid siren. Then they heard the throb of the engines of the bombers. Dogs howled. Small fire bombs clattered on roofs. Big bombs sounded like tearing sheets. Then came the crash of houses blowing up; the thud of walls falling down, the sound of fire alarms and the crackle of flames. Added to this was the hard ack-ack noise of the anti-aircraft guns as they tried to blow the German bombers out of the sky.

Blackout, sirens and shelters

The government ordered a blackout. No street lights, no shop lights, thick curtains at every window, covered traffic lights and no lighting cigarettes in the street. (Some people did wonder whether pilots could really see a lighted cigarette from an aeroplane).

Air raid sirens were put on top of tall buildings. They were switched on when German planes were spotted. Sandbags were put round buildings and people built air-raid shelters in their gardens or hid under tables indoors.

About 40,000 people died in the raids on London, Coventry, Glasgow and other cities.

B SOURCE

The warden shouted "Get in your shelters." I can't remember the sound, just the tumbling walls, the dust, and then the night sky. Our house had vanished.

Told to Fiona Reynoldson by Gerald Cole.

A SOURCE

How much sleep did you get last night?

None	Less than 4 hours	4–6 hours	More than 6 hours
31%	32%	22%	15%

C

A bus in a bomb crater in London in 1940.

D

People who have lived here all their lives don't know the way outside their doorsteps. I've never seen a place so beat – there's not a thing working.

A 'Mass Observation' report on Southampton in 1941. Mass Observation was set up to study how British people lived.

E

The centre of Coventry after heavy bombing.

Questions

1 Read the first paragraph.
   a What did Hitler decide to give up in September 1940?
   b What did he decide to do instead?

2 Read **The big bombers**. Copy the sentences below. Choose one of the words in *italics* each time there is a choice.
   The bombing started on 7 September. It went on for *days/weeks/months*. Every night people heard the *cry/shout/wail* of the air-raid siren. The next thing they heard was the throb of the engines of the *beachballs/bombers*. Often people heard small firebombs clatter on the *roof/wardens/cats*. The bombs had different *saddles/swords/sounds*. The *baby/big/bad* bombs sounded like tearing sheets. Houses crashed down, fire alarms went off and flames *crunched/cackled/crackled*. Added to all this was the noise of the *ack-ack/peck-peck* guns trying to shoot down the German *bats/bombers*.

THE ERA OF THE SECOND WORLD WAR 51

4.7 Propaganda

Propaganda

Propaganda is a sort of advertising. Advertisements on television or in magazines tell us what to buy. In wartime, governments use propaganda to tell us what to do. Governments sell the war as a good idea. Then everyone will fight hard. Propaganda can be a leaflet, poster, newspaper story, a film or on radio.

Russian propaganda

Everyone used propaganda in the war. For instance, the Russian government wanted all Russians to fight the Germans. They made a postcard of Hitler as a gorilla behind bars and sent thousands of these postcards to all the soldiers fighting.

British propaganda

At the beginning of the war the British dropped twelve million leaflets from aeroplanes which flew over Germany. The leaflets were written in German. They told the Germans how bad the war would be for them. They should give up now.

Radio and cinema

All the sides fighting made radio broadcasts. They said how good their side was or how bad the other side was. They all made films too. The films made their side look very brave. They made the other side look very bad.

SOURCE A

A Nazi poster of Hitler. It says 'One people, one empire, one leader'.

B When you lie, tell big lies.

From A. Bullock, 'Hitler a Study in Tyranny', 1952.

SOURCE C During a war news must be carefully controlled. Some news should not be made public.

From the diaries of Joseph Goebbels, Hitler's minister of propaganda.

D **SOURCE**

TYPES OF PROPAGANDA IN THE WAR

To keep their own people cheerful, and to depress the enemy, both sides changed the way they reported things. The type of propaganda they used varied.

The same report can be given in three different ways:

WHITE PROPAGANDA (The True Story):
We fought a tough battle on Tuesday. Both sides lost about 5,000 men. We only just won.

GREY PROPAGANDA (Half Truths):
We won a victory on Tuesday. We fought hard and finally beat the enemy. It was a long and fierce battle. The enemy lost about 5,000 men.

BLACK PROPAGANDA (Lies):
We beat the enemy again on Tuesday. It was an easy victory. We killed 20,000 of the enemy. Their soldiers ran away. We only lost 50 of our own men.

E **SOURCE**

As well as the BBC the British ran 'black propaganda' stations. They were not concerned with the truth. They pretended to be German radio stations. They told all sorts of lies about the German leaders. (The British wanted to get the Germans to hate their leaders.)

From Fiona Reynoldson, 'Propaganda', 1990.

F **SOURCE**

A Russian poster of Hitler from the Second World War.

Propaganda was used in various ways during the Second World War.

Questions

1 Read **Propaganda**. Fill in the gaps.
Propaganda is a sort of ____. Adverts tell us what to ____. In wartime governments use ____ to tell people what to do. They want to make everyone fight ____.

2 Write down the things from the following list that could be used as propaganda.
posters   films   flowerpots
air raids   books   banks   trees
leaflets   burgers   radio   food

3 Read Source A carefully. Read the caption.
   a What message is the poster trying to get over?
   b How does the poster do this?

4 Look at Source F carefully. Read the caption.
   a What message is the poster trying to get over?
   b How does it do this?

5 Look at Source D. Think up some propaganda of your own. Choose something like a pop group. Write a sentence about it. Turn the sentence into white, then grey, then black propaganda.

4.8 Why Did the Allies Win?

The war ended in 1945. By then the Allies were America, Britain, Russia and France. The Allies won. Why did they win? There are many possible reasons. The main ones are below.

- America was rich and had lots of guns.
- Britain didn't give in.
- Hitler invaded Russia and lost a lot of soldiers.
- Japan did not destroy the American aircraft carriers at Pearl Harbor.
- The Americans were so angry about Pearl Harbor that they declared war on Japan.
- Russia was big and had lots of weapons.
- Germany was surrounded.

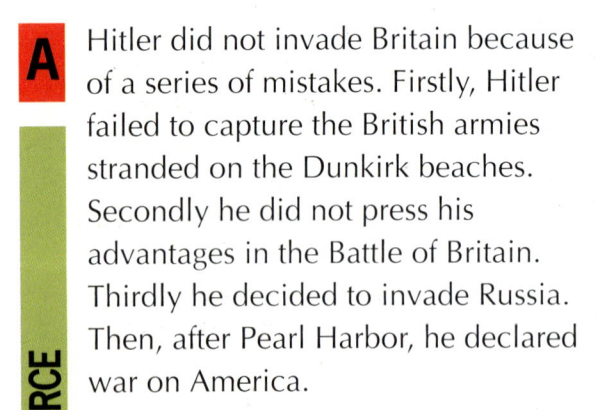

A Hitler did not invade Britain because of a series of mistakes. Firstly, Hitler failed to capture the British armies stranded on the Dunkirk beaches. Secondly he did not press his advantages in the Battle of Britain. Thirdly he decided to invade Russia. Then, after Pearl Harbor, he declared war on America.

SOURCE

From 'A Map History of the Modern World', 1982.

B We shall defend our island, whatever the cost may be. We shall fight on the beaches, we shall fight on the landing grounds, we shall fight in the field and in the street, we shall fight in the hills. We shall never surrender.

SOURCE

From a speech made by Winston Churchill in 1940.

C

SOURCE

An American playing card, showing Hitler being made a fool of by Russia.

D

SOURCE

A British cartoon from 1943, showing the Russian symbols (a hammer and sickle) destroying the Nazis forces.

54 · The Era of the Second World War

SOURCE E

Tanks 96,000

Aircraft 300,000

Artillery guns 61,000

Lorries 2,000,000

Rifles 7,000,000

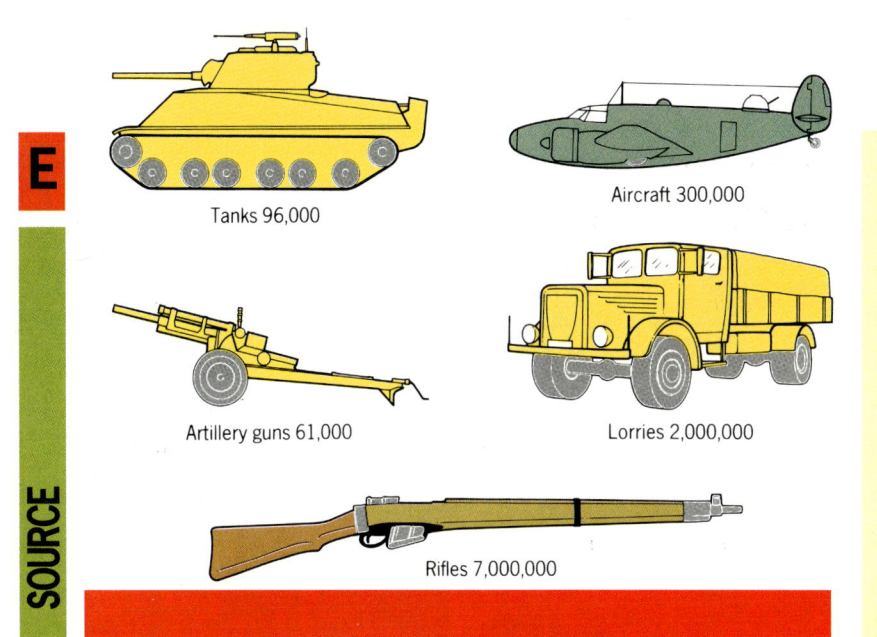

What America produced for the war 1940-45.

SOURCE F

America organized a scheme called 'lend-lease', by which Britain could borrow or hire American weapons. The President said it was like lending your garden hose to a neighbour whose house was on fire.

America lent billions of dollars' worth of weapons and goods to Britain and Russia between 1941-45. From C. Culpin, 'Making History', 1984.

SOURCE G

Neither the US (American) fleet nor US morale was destroyed by the attack on Pearl Harbor. America went to war. Churchill wrote, "So we have won after all."

N. Kelly, 'The Second World War', 1989.

SOURCE H

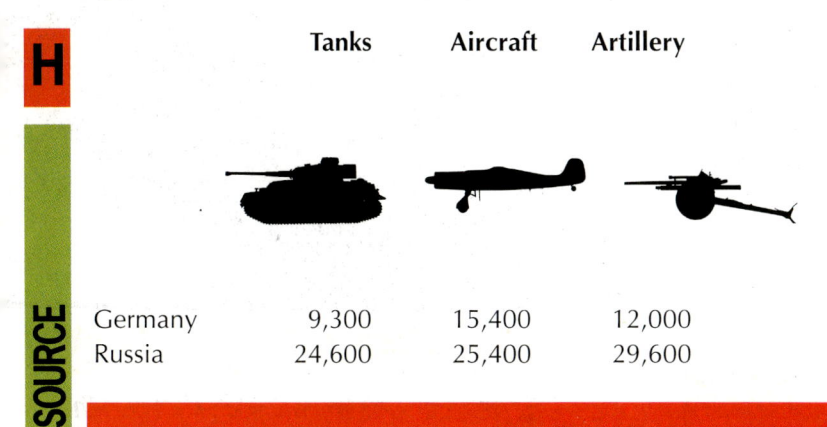

	Tanks	Aircraft	Artillery
Germany	9,300	15,400	12,000
Russia	24,600	25,400	29,600

The weapons that Germany and Russia made in just one year (1942).

Questions

1. Read the first paragraph. Write down the names of the four countries that were the Allies in 1945.

2. a Write down the main reasons why the Allies won the war.
   b Do you think any one reason is more important than the others. Explain why you think this.

3. Look at Source E.
   a How many rifles did America produce during the war?
   b What do you think they used the lorries for?

4. Look at Source H.
   a How many tanks did Russia make in 1942?
   b How can you tell that from 1942 onwards Russia was winning the war against Germany?

5. Read Source B.
   Choose the sentence below that best describes what Winston Churchill was saying.
   Germany is too strong for us.
   We shall not surrender.
   We shall not fight to the end.
   We shall hide in the hills.

THE ERA OF THE SECOND WORLD WAR 55

4.9 The Big Four

Franklin Delano Roosevelt

Born: 30 January 1882, Hyde Park, New York, America

Educated: Groton private school and Harvard University

Career Details:
- 1907 Began work as lawyer
- 1910 Elected as Democrat to New York state senate
- 1928 Elected Governor of New York
- 1932 Elected President of America
- 1936 Re-elected President
- 1940 Re-elected President
- 1944 Re-elected President

Health Problems: 1921 crippled by poliomyelitis. After three years treatment and exercise regained partial use of legs.

Death: 12 April 1945 as a result of stroke.

What he did:
- 1940 Sent help to Britain
- 1941 Brought America into the war
- 1942 Had talks with Britain and Russia on how to win the war

Adolf Hitler

Born: 20 April 1889, Branau am Inn, Austria

Educated: Local school. (Left at sixteen without qualifications.) Unsuccessful application to attend Vienna Academy of Fine Arts

Career Details:
- 1905–7 Lived at home with mother
- 1907–13 Lived in poverty in Vienna. Painted postcards and advertising posters
- 1914 Joined German army. Rose to rank of Corporal. In hospital when the First World War ended
- 1921 Became leader of Nazi Party (also called the National Socialist Party)
- 1924 Imprisoned following unsuccessful attempt to take over government of Munich
- 1933 Became Chancellor of Germany

Death: Committed suicide 30 April 1945

What he did:
Gave Germany a big army
Made lots of jobs for Germans
Got more land for Germany
Ran the war

Joseph Stalin

Born: Tiflis, Georgia, Russia, 21 December 1879
(Real name Joseph Vissarionovich Djugashvili)

Educated: Local school and priests' training college (expelled 1899 for joining in revolutionary activities)

Career Details:

1902 Arrested for revolutionary activity and sent into exile in Siberia – escaped
1905–8 Organized bank raids to raise money for revolutionary Bolshevik (later Communist) Party
1922 Became Secretary of the Communist Party
1924 Following death of Communist leader, Lenin, Stalin gradually came to control all of Russia
1941 Became Premier of Russia

Death: 6 March 1953

What he did:
Made Russia more modern
1939 Signed Nazi–Soviet Pact with Germany to buy time to build up the Russian army
1941 Took control of fighting against Germany
Encouraged the Russian people in the war effort
Talked with the British and the Americans about how to win the war

Winston Churchill

Born: Blenheim Palace, Oxford, England 30 November 1874

Educated: Harrow School and Sandhurst Military Academy

Career Details:
Joined army and took part in Battle of Omdurman
1898 Worked as journalist during Boer War
1900 Became Conservative MP
1904 Joined Liberal Party
1910 Became Home Secretary
1922 Lost seat as MP
1924 Elected as Conservative MP
1924–9 Became Chancellor of the Exchequer
1940 Became Prime Minister

Death: 24 January 1965

What he did:
Spoke out in the 1930s about not giving in to Hitler
Ran the wartime government
Encouraged the British people to fight
Talked with the Americans and the Russians about how to win the war

Questions

1 Copy the following sentences. Choose one of the words in *italics* each time there is a choice.

Roosevelt
Roosevelt was born in *1982/1882*. He was elected President of America *six/four* times. He brought America into the *war/peace*.

Hitler
Hitler was born in *1889/1899*. In 1921 he became leader of the *Nasty/Nazi/Daisy* Party. In 1933 he became Chancellor of *Italy/Germany*.

Stalin
Stalin was born in *1809/1879*. In 1941 he became leader of *Russia/France*.

Churchill
Churchill was born in *1874/1784*. He became a *Communist/Conservative* MP in 1900. He became Prime Minister in *1849/1940/1999*. He encouraged the British people to *surrender/fight*.

2 Which three men met to talk about how to win the war?

5.1 A Divided Europe

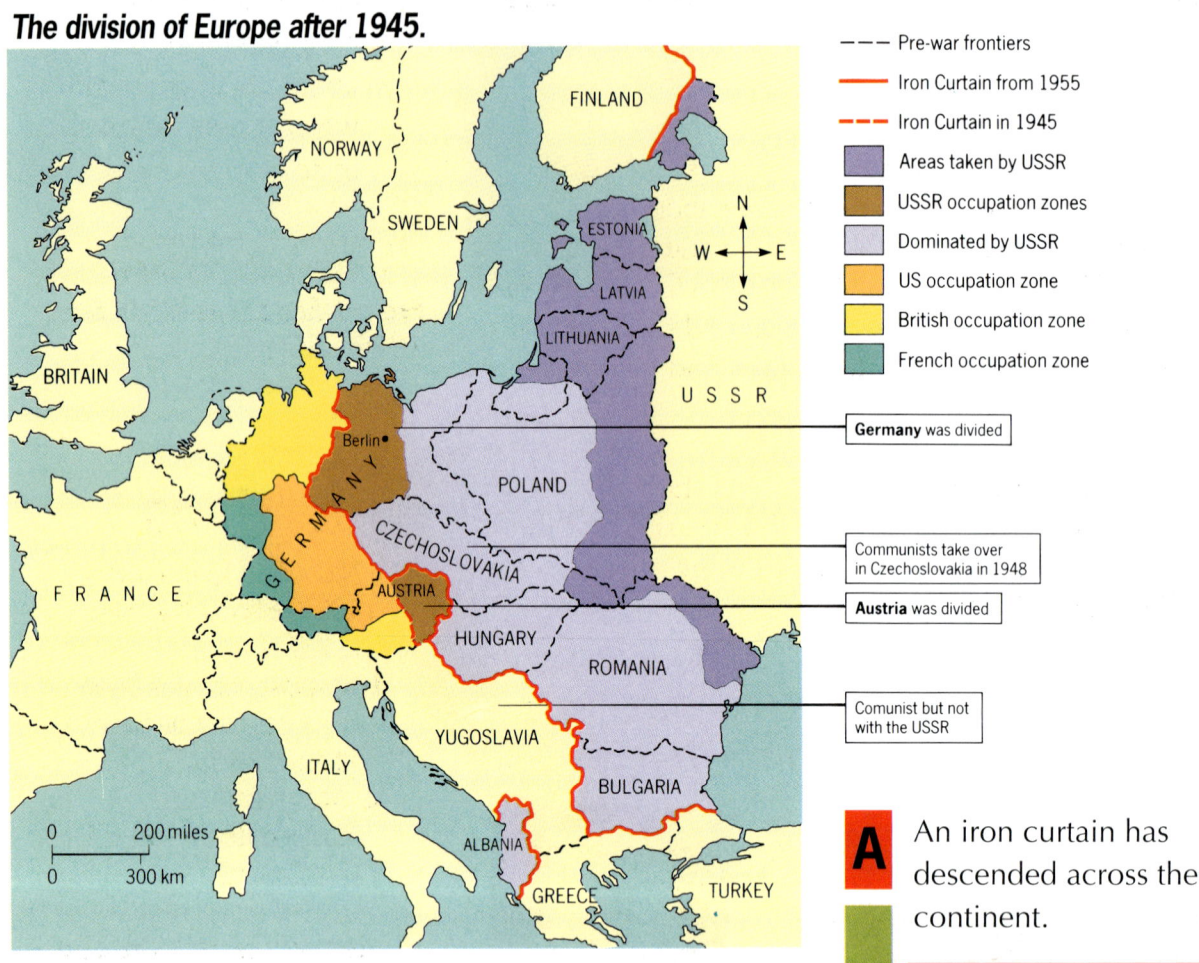

The division of Europe after 1945.

Map legend:
- – – – Pre-war frontiers
- —— Iron Curtain from 1955
- – – – Iron Curtain in 1945
- Areas taken by USSR
- USSR occupation zones
- Dominated by USSR
- US occupation zone
- British occupation zone
- French occupation zone

Map annotations:
- **Germany** was divided
- Communists take over in Czechoslovakia in 1948
- **Austria** was divided
- Comunist but not with the USSR

The last German soldiers surrendered on 7 May 1945.

The Allies meet

The Allies were Britain, America, France and Russia. They had won the war. They divided Germany into four **zones**. There was one for each of the Allies (see map). Berlin was Germany's capital city. It was divided into four zones as well.

The Allies argue

Russia never wanted to be invaded again. So the Russians grabbed as much land as they could. Look at the map on this page. All the mauve and purple land was controlled by the Russians. It made a buffer or block between them and

A An iron curtain has descended across the continent.

Said by Winston Churchill in a speech in America, in 1946.

B As early as 1941 Stalin had made it clear that Russia would only allow friendly countries on its borders. He said that twice in thirty years Russia had been invaded through an unfriendly Poland.

L. Snellgrove, 'The Modern World Since 1870', 1981.

Germany. They said they were taking this land to make themselves safer, not because they were greedy for more land.

The Cold War

Although Russia had fought on the same side as Britain, France and America, they did not agree about how countries should be run. Britain, France and America believed in Democracy. Russia believed in Communism. In 1947 President Truman of America said he did not want to see Russia controlling any more land and making all the people be communists.

Although there was no fighting between the Allies there was bad feeling. The Russians were on one side and the Americans, British and French were on the other. This was called the Cold War.

C SOURCE By 1948 all the countries which Russia controlled had one-party governments which were controlled by the Communists.

From J. Scott, 'The World Since 1914', 1989.

Questions

1. Look at the map on page 58.
   a What colour is the British zone?
   b In whose zone was Berlin?
   c What colour is the line of the Iron Curtain?
   d Who controlled the countries to the east of the Iron Curtain?

2. Read the paragraph **The Cold War**.
   a Is the statement below true or false?
   'The Allies did not fight each other, but there was bad feeling.'
   b America, Britain and France were on one side in the Cold War. Which country was on the other side?

D SOURCE

The court at Nurenburg, where many Nazis were tried for 'war crimes'. Many were never caught or tried.

5.2 The United Nations Organization

Many countries were tired of war. They wanted peace. They wanted fewer guns in the world. They wanted better health for everyone. They wanted everyone to be free.

The United Nations Charter 1945

Just as the war was ending, many countries sent people to America. They talked about making a better world. Twenty-six signed the United Nations Charter (Source B).

The General Assembly

A special building was built in New York. It was called the United Nations Building. Men and women from every country that joined met in a big hall in the building. They talked about how they would make the world a better place to live in. When all the members met it was called the **General Assembly**.

B (SOURCE)

1. Against war.
2. Defend the worth of all people.
3. Equal rights for men and women and all countries.
4. Respect treaties.
5. Improve world-wide standards of living.

The main beliefs of the United Nations Charter, 1945.

C (SOURCE)

The League of Nations thought that all nations would put the good of the world first, before their own interests.

The United Nations accepts that nations are greedy, selfish, and prepared to help others only as long as too much is not demanded of them.

From P. Moss, 'Modern World History', 1978.

A (SOURCE)

THE LEAGUE OF NATIONS	UNITED NATIONS
MANY IMPORTANT COUNTRIES, INCLUDING U.S.A., DID NOT JOIN	EVERY IMPORTANT NATION IS A MEMBER
A NUMBER OF NATIONS WALKED OUT WHEN THEY DID NOT AGREE	THERE IS NO PROVISION FOR A MEMBER TO LEAVE THE U.N. THOUGH MEMBERS MAY BE EXPELLED
THE LEAGUE HAD NO ARMED FORCE TO STOP WAR	MEMBERS PROVIDE SOLDIERS FOR SPECIAL TASKS

This cartoon compares the League of Nations with the United Nations. P. Moss, 'History Alive', 1977.

The Security Council

Five important countries were permanent members of the Security Council. These were America, Britain, Russia, China and France. Six other countries (later 10 other countries) sent members to sit on the Security Council for two years at a time. The Security Council met often and ran the United Nations.

The Right to Veto

All the five permanent members had a **veto**. For instance, if they voted on whether to send United Nations' soldiers to keep the peace in Korea and one of the five did not agree, then that one could say no. This no, or veto, meant that the soldiers would not be sent.

Some organizations run by the United Nations

- Court of International Justice
- Food and Agriculture Organization
- United Nations Education, Scientific and Cultural Organization
- World Health Organization
- United Nations Relief and Rehabilitation Administration
- International Refugee Organization

D SOURCE

The League failed for two reasons. First of all, powerful countries like America and Germany (after 1933) were not members. Secondly they had no way to make members keep the peace. The United Nations had most of the powerful nations as members. But it still had trouble getting them to do as they were told.

From J Scott, 'The World Since 1914', 1989.

Questions

1 Copy the following sentences, matching the Heads and Tails.

Many countries were	to be free.
They wanted everyone	tired of war.
They wanted world	to live well.
They wanted everyone	peace.

2 Read the paragraph **The United Nations Charter**. Read Source B.
   a Write down the main points of the Charter.
   b Design a poster to show what they were.

3 Look at Source A.
   In what three ways was the United Nations better than the League of Nations?

4 Read the last section and Sources B and D.
   a Why might the United Nations have trouble with Point 2 of the Charter?
   b Which organization might help people to reach Point 5 of the Charter?

5.3 Refugees

Refugees are people who have been forced to leave their homes.

The Second World War and refugees

The war was a world war so there were millions of refugees all over the world. Huge armies had fought with guns and tanks over miles and miles of land. Many homes were burnt or blown up. People ran away. Many Jews and others were forced to leave their homes during the war.

The Americans had bombed Japan so much that many Japanese had no homes. In China there were thousands and thousands of women, men and children who had lost their homes in the fighting with Japan.

Europe at the end of the war

Europe was a mess. The Russians advanced into Germany at the end of the war. Terrified Germans packed their bags and fled to the west. Millions of panic stricken refugees poured into the German ports on the Baltic Sea. They queued and fought to get on to ships as the Russian soldiers drew closer. Then, when the war was over, many countries like Poland were freed from German control. Lots of them hated the Germans. They threw them out of their countries. In all 16 million Germans and East Europeans trudged back towards Germany.

The United Nations

At the end of the war there were millions of refugees. The United Nations tried to help. It set up a group to help refugees. The group built camps and gave food and clothing. They helped people to make a new life. A great deal of the money for the camps and so on came from America. Most other countries had fought for so long that they had no money left.

A SOURCE
When I was in Berlin you could get any German to do anything for a bar of chocolate or a loaf of bread.

Told to Fiona Reynoldson in 1972, by a British soldier who had been in Berlin in 1945.

B SOURCE
By 1946 European food production was half its pre war level.

From 'The Times Atlas of the Second World War', 1989.

C SOURCE
Hitler's Germany employed slave labour in the factories, mines and farms. Thus the Germans shifted many people all over Europe.

From B. Catchpole, 'Map History of the Modern World', 1982.

D Chinese refugees in 1946.

E

16 million refugees trudged towards the west. Two million died.

F The Wilhelm Gustloff was a big ship. Normally it carried 1,900 people. On the night of 30 January 1945, 8,000 refugees crowded on board. A Russian submarine spotted the ship making its way through the choppy ice cold sea. The ship was torpedoed and sunk. Everyone died.

From Fiona Reynoldson, 'Evacuees', 1990.

Questions

1. Read the first sentence. What is a refugee?

2. Read the paragraph **Europe at the end of the war**.
   a. Who advanced into Germany at the end of the war?
   b. How many refugees went back to Germany?

3. Design a poster asking for help for refugees. What would they need? (food, jobs....)

4. Read Source F.
   a. How many people was the ship supposed to carry?
   b. How many was it carrying when it sank?
   c. Who were the refugees running away from?
   d. Many more Germans died in this disaster than on the *Titanic*. Yet we know more about the Titanic. Choose the most likely reason for this from the list below.

   They story was made up.
   The Germans lost the war, so no one cared if they died.
   Lots of refugees were dying everywhere.
   No journalists reported it.

THE ERA OF THE SECOND WORLD WAR 63

INDEX

Abyssinia 18–19
Africa 9, 18
Albania 26
Allies 7, 34, 41, 54, 58–59
America 8–10, 32, 34, 36–37, 48, 54–55, 58–62
Anarchists 20
appeasement 24–25
Aryan people 42
atomic bomb 36–37
Austria 7, 22–23
Austria-Hungary 7

Battle of Britain 29
Berlin 35, 43, 58, 62
blackout 28
Blitz 29, 50
Blitzkrieg 28
Britain 10, 13, 17, 19, 21, 24, 26–29, 32, 34, 38, 46, 50, 54, 55, 58–59, 61
Canada 48
Caucasus 30
Chamberlain 24–25
China 14–15, 61–62
Churchill, Winston 17, 24, 54–55, 57–58
cinema 52
Cold War 59
Cologne 35
Communist 10–12, 20–21, 59
Concentration camps 43–45
Coral Sea 36
Court of International Justice 61
Czechoslovakia 24–26

D-Day 34, 41
Democratic 10, 59
Denmark 28
Dresden 35
Dunkirk 28–29

El Alamein 34
evacuation 48–49

Far East 32–33, 36
Fascist 10–12, 18
Finland 8
First World War 4–5, 7–8, 17, 24
France 5, 7, 10, 13, 17, 19, 21, 24, 26–29, 34, 38–39, 41, 54, 58–59, 61
Franco, General 20–21

gas masks 28
Germany 5, 7, 9–10, 13, 16–17, 19–30, 34–35, 38–39, 41–43, 52, 54–55, 58–59, 61–62
Gestapo 39
Ghettoes 44

Hamburg 35
Hiroshima 36–37
Hitler, Adolf 10–13, 16–17, 19, 21–24, 26–27, 29–31, 35, 39, 42, 43–44, 50, 52–54, 56, 62
Holocaust 42, 44
Home Front 46
Home Guard 47

Italy 10, 11, 13, 17–19, 21, 23, 26, 34

Japan 9, 14–15, 32, 36–37, 54, 62
Jews 42–44, 62

kamikazes 36

League of Nations 8–9, 14–17, 19, 22, 60
left-wing 20–21
Lithuania 9, 26
Luftwaffe 29

Maginot Line 28
Malaya 32
Mediterranean Sea 34
Middle East 9, 34
Midway 37
Mosley, Oswald 13
Mussolini, Benito 10–13, 18–19, 21, 23

Nagasaki 37
National Socialist Party 16
Nazi Party 13, 16, 23, 42, 43
Nazi-Soviet Pact 26
Norway 28, 39

Pacific Ocean 32
pacifists 5
Pearl Harbor 33, 54–55
Philippines 32
Phoney War 28
Picasso 20
Poland 26–28, 62
propaganda 52

radio 52–53
RAF 29
rascism 12
rationing 46
refugees 62–63
Resistance 41
Rhineland 22
Roosevelt, Franklin D 56
Russia 5, 7, 9–10, 21, 26, 28, 30, 34, 38, 54–55, 58–59

Saar 16–17
Singapore 33

sirens 50
Socialist 20–21
Spain 20–21
Spanish Civil War 20–21
Special Operations Executive (SOE) 41
SS (Schutz-Staffeln) 39, 44
Stalin 27, 57–58
Stalingrad 30–31
Sudetenland 24–25
Suez Canal 34
Sweden 8

Tokyo 36
Treaty of Versailles 7
Turkey 7

United Nations 60–62

Von Paulus 31
Von Schuschnigg 23

Warsaw 28
Women 4, 30, 41, 46–47
Women's Land Army 47
Women's Voluntary Service 47
Woodrow Wilson 8–9
World Health Organization 61